T0194964

Gospel Commands for Living a Good Life

A New Testament View of the Ten Commandments

Mara Jane Cawein, PhD

Better known as
Doctor Grammy

WESTBOW
PRESS®
A DIVISION OF THOMAS NELSON
& ZONDERVAN

This book is a work of non-fiction. Unless otherwise noted, the author
and the publisher make no explicit guarantees as to the accuracy of
the information contained in this book and in some cases, names of
people and places have been altered to protect their privacy.

WestBow Press books may be ordered through booksellers or by contacting:

WestBow Press
A Division of Thomas Nelson & Zondervan
1663 Liberty Drive
Bloomington, IN 47403
www.westbowpress.com
1 (866) 928-1240

Because of the dynamic nature of the Internet, any web addresses or
links contained in this book may have changed since publication and
may no longer be valid. The views expressed in this work are solely those
of the author and do not necessarily reflect the views of the publisher,
and the publisher hereby disclaims any responsibility for them.

Any people depicted in stock imagery provided by Getty Images are
models, and such images are being used for illustrative purposes only.
Certain stock imagery © Getty Images.

Scripture taken from the New King James Version®. Copyright © 1982
by Thomas Nelson. Used by permission. All rights reserved.

ISBN: 978-1-9736-8285-1 (sc)
ISBN: 978-1-9736-8287-5 (hc)
ISBN: 978-1-9736-8286-8 (e)

Library of Congress Control Number: 2020900463

Print information available on the last page.

WestBow Press rev. date: 01/20/2020

Contents

Foreword

When I first met Dr. Cawein as a sophomore in the Honors College at the University of Central Arkansas, I was unaware of the support she would give me two years later for my capstone project required for graduating with honors. I quickly became aware of her faith in education classes required for the middle-level education program. She told students that her last name rhymed with "tall pine," but beyond this, I could tell that she believed; she loved God. She knew the necessity of bringing faith into every aspect of her life. She was not ashamed and crafted a platform on which students could confidently allow faith to seep into their education. We agreed that Jesus' life should be reflected in everything, including our jobs.

In one of her classes, I presented on the power that praise has on students and communicated the connection to Ephesians 4:29, "Let no corrupt word proceed out of your mouth, but what is good for necessary edification, that it may impart grace to the hearers." I began drawing a series of connections between God-given instructions and current research on educational theories. Through a number of instances such as this, my capstone project developed into an attempt to bridge the gap between Jesus as a teacher and modern pedagogical strategies.

In short, my project argued that learner centered approaches, both proven effective by current research and used in twenty-first century classrooms, are not far from the strategies used by Jesus. Perhaps Jesus' methods can provide valuable information, especially for Christian educators. My stake in this project was as deep as it was wide. I sought to place Jesus and education, two topics I am highly passionate about, together in such a way that my own, as well as others', teaching philosophies might be influenced. Beyond this, an even greater stake existed—that of my own relationship with Jesus! Ephesians 2:8-10 states, "For by grace you have been saved through faith, and that not of yourselves; it is the gift of God, not of works, lest anyone should boast. For we are His workmanship, created in Christ Jesus for good works, which God prepared beforehand that we should walk in them." Convinced that this project was a "good work" that God prepared beforehand that I might walk in it, I needed a mentor that knew the weight that it held in my heart.

In parallel to the way I sought to bring together Jesus' methods with teaching strategies of today, Dr. Cawein's book seems to connect two lines—between the life of Jesus and how we ought to live ours. C.S. Lewis wrote, "I believe in Christianity as I believe that the Sun has risen, not only because I see it but because by it, I see everything else." Dr. Cawein views living a good life through the lens of her beliefs in Christ as her Savior. My hope and prayer for her readers is that they are challenged and encouraged by the life of Jesus and the ways in which it changes ours. I know my life was changed by Dr. Cawein; beyond that, I know each of ours has been changed by His. Might yours be as well?

Madison Breazeale Smith
Cru Campus Ministry at the University of Central Arkansas

Preface

My first question as a newly retired teacher was simple: "How should I live the rest of my life?" I have always tried to live well but felt a special urgency in this new stage of retirement. Therefore, my first retirement project became a quest to determine how one should go about living a good life. Since I had a rewarding career in education, I decided to pursue the answer to this question using academic tools. The research that follows has been an intellectually and spiritually enriching experience for me. I used what I have learned as an analyst with a math degree, a researcher with a PhD in leadership studies from the University of Central Arkansas, and a Christian who has faithfully studied the Bible. I decided to study the life of Jesus using scripture as my primary source of information. Jesus Christ was the only perfect example of living well. Therefore, I used the four gospels of the Bible (Matthew, Mark, Luke, and John) as the best firsthand accounts of Jesus' life as the Son of Man. I was pleasantly surprised at how much I learned from my in-depth analysis of the gospels. I hope the following pages will inspire others to live a better life.

In this project, I used qualitative analysis of the four gospels of Matthew, Mark, Luke, and John. I have always been drawn to grounded theory in my study of research methods, so I used this approach as I coded, memoed, and analyzed the gospels as my primary data source. After careful reading, themes began to emerge. I then researched other sources, beginning with the other books of the Bible, religious writings, including commentaries of the Bible, favorite gospel songs, and current research related to my findings. My research questions were, "How should people live? Does the life of Jesus tell us anything about how we should live in today's world? If Jesus is the only perfect and good human being, then can His life also inform our lives?"

I originally intended for this project to be more secular in its findings, hoping that anyone could use this regardless of religious affiliation. However, as I delved more deeply into the gospels, they were so spiritual that I could not ignore that aspect of human existence. The human spirit cannot be ignored; it exists separate from our worldly selves. Our spirit must be fed just as our bodies need food. If we do not follow Jesus, then our souls yearn for a less-perfect substitute. This project has helped me focus on living a better life, and I hope it helps my dear readers as well.

Mara Jane Cawein, PhD
Better known as
Doctor Grammy

CHAPTER 1

Seek a Better Life

God is Spirit: and those who worship Him must worship in spirit and truth.

—John 4:24

It is the very nature of life to strive to continue in being. Since this continuance can be secured only by constant renewals, life is a self-renewing process.

—John Dewey

How does one live a good life? I began to research this question with intensity upon entering retirement. As a youngster, I thought I was good if I obeyed my parents. As I grew older, my teachers seemed to know all the answers, so I was compliant. Then I entered the teaching profession and realized that I did not have all the answers but only helped others find answers for themselves. In addition to required curriculum, I kept three reference books that I felt were necessary in my mathematics classroom. The first was a book of mathematical formulas. The second was a dictionary. The third was the Bible. The Bible got the most use. Even though I worked in a public school, students had serious questions about life. I tried my best to answer each and every one without preaching but by just pointing them in the right direction. I remember one particular class that asked many deep questions, and frequently, we had deep discussions before getting into the lesson. Various topics included the price of high school rings, the lack of drinking fountains near my classroom, the Vietnam War, and the meaning of life. I think after I had answered many previous questions well, the student was half-joking when she asked me for the meaning of life. I must have surprised her when I quickly answered by telling her to read Ecclesiastes.

Ecclesiastes was written by Solomon, arguably the wisest human. The Preacher in the book provides a short version of his search for the meaning of life. "I, the Preacher, was king over Israel in Jerusalem, and I set my heart to seek and search out by wisdom concerning all that is done under heaven; this burdensome task God has given to the sons of man, by which they may be exercised" (Ecclesiastes 1:12–13). In chapter 7, he continues to ask the reader to not be overly righteous since all sin and fall short of perfection. His brief summation is in the final two verses of chapter 12, "Let us hear the conclusion of the whole matter: Fear God and keep His commandments, for this is man's all. For God will bring every work into judgement, including every secret thing, whether good or evil."

The commandments at that time were the Ten Commandments given to Moses in Exodus 20. Most people know briefly what these say, but many question them today for two reasons. First, we are becoming an increasingly secular society. Some people are even offended by religious writings, especially overtly Christian writings. Second, they were written very long ago, and many feel that the New Testament erases the laws given in the Old Testament. I will address these two concerns and then explain the organization of the rules for living a good life based on the Ten Commandments.

For those who prefer the secular over religious answers, should they care about the Ten Commandments in the Bible? John Dewey, an esteemed educator known and appreciated by most who study education and perhaps those who do not, studied how to best provide education in a democratic society. Not everyone is religious, but all people need to review and renew their spirits if they are going to grow and improve their lives. John Dewey confirmed the need for renewal in our lives, and he may have been talking about renewal of the human spirit. We are creatures who love to learn; our brains want to work. Renewal is part of our nature. Some find renewal in nature or art. My prayer is that you will allow yourself to be renewed by the Holy Spirit through divine ventures: Bible reading, prayer, and Christian fellowship. Even if you want to avoid praise and worship of a higher being, six of the Ten Commandments may still speak to you. The nonreligious may want to skim past chapters 2 through 5, which are the ones about loving God. The next involve being kind and loving toward our neighbors, which is much easier to do with belief in a loving God.

For those who are religious, there is still the argument that the Old Testament does not apply to today's world. For them, I looked at the gospels of the New Testament for my primary data. I also looked at the other books of the Bible as well as other sources but only after a careful analysis of the four gospels as I searched for the answer to living a good life. Even many who are not Christian recognize Jesus Christ as a master teacher, a philosopher, and even a prophet. For nearly two thousand years, our dating system recognized the life-changing actions of this Son of Man or Son of God, depending on your perspective. Throughout my education, dates were either BC ("before Christ") or AD (*anno Domini*, "In the year of our Lord"). Even though the Christian references are gone with the use of CE ("of the Common Era") and BCE ("before the Common Era"), the life of Jesus is still the dividing point.

What do the gospels share about righteous living? In two of the gospels (Matthew 22:34–40, Mark 12:28–34), one of the teachers of the Jewish law asks Jesus to state the most important commandment. The following chapters can be summarized by Jesus' answer to first love God with all your heart, soul, mind, and strength. The second proceeds from the first—love your neighbor as yourself. I had originally wanted to concentrate on the second command, but after analyzing the gospels, I could not ignore the spiritual side of living well. Humans cannot live well without addressing the needs of the human spirit. If the spirit is not fed, it gets thirsty. Perhaps it is not surprising that my academic analysis produced spiritual data that could not be ignored since the Bible was my primary data source.

Scripture, which for me includes both the Old Testament and New Testament of the Bible, has been a key source of spiritual renewal for me. I have not memorized much of the Bible, but I do know that the Lord is my shepherd, as shared in the beloved Psalm 23. God has good things in store for us if we will accept them. When we give our allegiance to God, He sends a Spirit of Truth to guide us (John 16:13). This was a key theme in Charles M. Sheldon's book *In His Steps*. This book sparked a movement of Christians vowing to live their lives with Jesus as their example, asking "What Would Jesus Do?" or WWJD. I wore one of the plastic bracelets for a while. The perfect example of Jesus' life has been a powerful force for goodness in my life as well as in the world.

Jesus relied on scripture as He taught and preached. He used the law and the prophets, including Isaiah, Moses, and others (with a short list provided in Appendix B). Jesus only had the Old Testament of the Bible, but He held it in reverence as a source of truth and of comfort. In fact, when tempted in the desert after His baptism, He found support from scripture as the devil's temptations were refuted. Jesus said, "It is written, Man shall not live by bread alone, but by every word that proceeds from the mouth of God" (Matthew 4:4). As shared in Psalm 119, all scripture is valuable for living a righteous and fulfilling life. Spiritual food can be found in the Old Testament as well as the New Testament. Jesus stated in Matthew 5:17, "Do not think that I came to destroy the Law or the Prophets. I did not come to destroy but to fulfil." Jesus acknowledged the value of scripture, which in His day was the Old Testament—often referred to as the law and the prophets. After Jesus' baptism and before His public ministry, He was tempted by the devil. He used scripture to answer all three temptations. Perhaps solid knowledge of the Bible could help all of us make good decisions when we are faced with life-changing experiences, opportunities, and temptations. Jesus did not replace the Old Testament teachings but allowed scripture to guide His life. With the guidance of scripture, He was able to show us how to live. "For the law was given through Moses, but grace and truth came through Jesus Christ" (John 1:17).

I have found great comfort and direction in scripture at various times of my life. I have always kept a Bible handy at work and tried to read from it at least once a day. One day, my husband had forgotten to do something that was very important to me. I was mad. As I approached my Bible reading, my heart was troubled. God led me to a verse that I truly needed at the time, Psalm 66:18 (Coincidently, eighteen was my programmer number at the time.): "If I regard iniquity in my heart, the Lord will not hear." It was amazing how quickly I forgave him and felt at peace after reading that. The Bible truly has a supernatural power to put my mind at ease. Troubles do not always disappear, but I am always able to face times of trouble with God's help.

My goal in writing this book is to discover the pathway to live a good life. The Bible is my source of spiritual strength. I pray that all readers find their own path to spiritual renewal.

> So that you incline your ear to wisdom, and apply your heart to understanding; yes, if you cry out for discernment, and lift up your voice for understanding, if you seek her as silver, and search for her as for hidden treasures; then you will understand the fear of the Lord, and find the knowledge of God. For the Lord gives wisdom; from His mouth come knowledge and understanding. (Proverbs 2:2–6)

The following chapters contain the commands I have uncovered after my careful analysis of the four gospels. In each chapter, keywords from the gospels led me to the commands, and then scripture from the Old and New Testaments testifies to its truth. I have also found evidence of the truth in my own experiences and through further research of more current academic and philosophical knowledge. These commands are based on the two commands from Jesus: love God and love your neighbor. As I was organizing and analyzing the keywords, they surprisingly matched well with the ten commandments of the Old Testament. This will be noted further in my conclusion. Note that the first four of the Ten Commandments refer to how we should love God. These are the basis of the next four chapters. The remaining six commandments relate to how we should interact with our neighbors. This will be the basis for chapters 6 through 11. Although the Ten Commandments show us how to act, the fulfillment of those commands in the New Testament add compassion so we can love one another in spirit and in truth. It is not enough to do the right thing; God requires a clean heart as well. Although only one human was fully good, God's Son, Jesus, I hope that the following chapters help you on your journey to perfection through our Lord, Jesus Christ.

Each chapter will begin with a key gospel verse and a relevant quote from more recent times. Throughout, I have used the New King James Version because it is my favorite translation at this time in my life. After I explain the command for righteous living using the gospels, the entire Bible, current knowledge, and my personal experiences, you will find the following for further meditation: key Bible verses, keywords from the gospels, a Christian song, and questions for personal reflection.

– ❦ –

Key Bible Verses: Psalm 119, John 1:1, 2 John 6

Keywords: fulfil(led), ghost, law, prophet(s), scripture(s), spirit(s), tradition, word(s), written

Song: "Thy Word (is a lamp onto my feet and a light unto my path)"

Questions:

1. What is your favorite Bible verse?

2. Where do you find your spiritual food? Some people may find it in songs, others in nature or creative works that include art and books. What do you do on a regular basis for your spiritual needs?

3. When things go wrong, how do you react? Where do you find strength in times of trouble?

Ponderable:

While finishing this project, I found a quote by the now-late President George H. W. Bush. Do you agree with this kind man who has become the longest living president up to now?

Lincoln said you cannot be President without spending some time on your knees. I have repeated that and a bunch of Atheists got all over me. Wait a minute. Does that mean that you cannot be President if you are an Atheist? I say yea that does mean that.[1]

---

[1] From *https://www.brainyquote.com/quotes/george_h_w_bush_464503*.

CHAPTER 2

Choose Your Master

No servant can serve two masters; for either he will hate the one and love the other; or else he will be loyal to the one and despise the other. Ye cannot serve God and mammon.

—Luke 16:13

Let us choose wisely the course we will follow.

—Carol Swain

Alumni brick on UCA campus

Ultimately, life comes down to making choices. Our choice to do nothing is a choice. Our choice to do what we are told is also a choice. What guides you in your choices? Do you go with the flow or consider every choice carefully? Choices also have varying degrees of impact. Some are life changing while others are just a matter of personal preference. Choose well. Making good choices has been a common theme for me as a teacher, and thus I included this phrase on my alumni brick for my bachelor of science degree at the University of Central Arkansas (UCA). The most important choice in life is who or what to follow, as it guides all future choices.

The first of the Ten Commandments is, "I am the Lord your God, who brought you out of the land of Egypt, out of the house of bondage. You shall have no other gods before Me" (Exodus 20:2–3). One must choose God above all other gods, which include the gods of money, sex, power, possessions, self-indulgence, drugs, etc. Some people claim they can be the master of their lives, but that path ultimately ends in ruin. Others may think they can serve two masters, loving God and loving the trappings of this world. Serving two masters leads to ruin. As stated in Luke 16:13, you will eventually be required to choose either God or the world.

As I read through the gospels, two themes seemed to emerge above all others: kingdom and choices. The frequency of kingdom talk convinced me that a good life must include the spiritual as well as human relationships. This chapter and the next three will address the spiritual side of living the good life. Of all the keywords that I analyzed, only *Father* occurred more often, with 244 instances, as compared to *kingdom,* with 124, followed closely by *see,* with 123, and *give,* with 119. God, our Father, is essential for living a good life since all good things come from Him. Choose God as your master in this world so that you may enjoy the next. John the Baptist implored others to change their ways and choose the good life offered by obedience to God. Matthew described him: "Saying 'Repent, for the kingdom of heaven is at hand!'. For this is he who was spoken of by the prophet Isaiah, saying: The voice of one crying in the wilderness: Prepare the way of the Lord; make His paths straight'" (Matthew 3:2–3). The kingdom is at hand and cannot be ignored.

The theme of binary choices surprised me because this world is so full of gray areas. There were no gray areas in the gospels, only choices between one way or another. These choices are evident in all four gospels. In Matthew 7:13–14, there are only two gates; many enter the wide one that leads toward destruction, but few enter the smaller gate that leads to life. In Matthew 25:2, there were ten virgins divided simply as five wise and five foolish. Please pray that you will be counted among the wise, not the foolish, for we will be divided in the end between the sheep and the goats (Matthew 25:32). The gospel of Mark exhorts us to follow the commands of God, not rules or traditions of men (Mark 7:7–8), for it will do you no good if you gain the whole world but lose your soul (Mark 8:36). In Mark 10:6, all of humanity is divided as either male or female. I fear that the gender confusion is a temptation of the world rather than the purposeful creation of God. Luke's gospel contains many binary choices as well: the disciples left their earthly belongings to follow Jesus (Luke 5:28); a candle cannot be covered and is either on or off (Luke 8:16); others are either for or against Jesus (Luke 9:50); and a great gulf divides the saved and unsaved in the afterlife (Luke 16:26). John declares that one must be born again to enter heaven (John 3:6). John continues with choices of doing good or doing evil (John 5:29), of working for food that spoils or food that endures (John 6:27), and of loving praise of men or of God (John 12:43). The gospel message is clear: one cannot straddle the fence and still gain eternal life.

Many of the gospel characters had serious choices to make. Joseph could have quietly divorced Mary but chose to protect her reputation and listen to his dream. John the Baptist called on his followers to repent and be baptized. Jesus asked His disciples to follow. We will eventually be judged as sheep or goats, on the right hand or the left, to eternal life or wailing and gnashing of teeth. We must choose either a life of following the life of Jesus Christ or allowing the world to control our choices. As Joshua said in the Old Testament, choose whom you will serve, today and every day thereafter. You cannot be a Christian and follow the ways of the world. No one can serve two masters.

We all make choices in our lives. Some of them alter our futures. I pray that everyone reading this will choose life in Jesus Christ and that every choice leads in that direction. Looking back, I realize that one of the best choices I ever made was to marry a man who was Christian, attended church, and put family before worldly pursuits. I was young, but my spirit knew that someone who attended family gatherings, played with younger nieces and nephews, and attended church services faithfully was a good catch. After forty-five years together (mostly good years), I have no regrets.

I Chose You

They said we were too young to really know about love.
They said to finish school.
Perhaps we were not yet mature, but I understood you.
I knew that you were very cool.

I chose my feelings toward you over a career, prestigious degrees.
I chose having your family over the temptations of the world
and have no regrets.

I now have you, a family, a degree, and a joy-filled Christian life.
I chose you and know that your love and leadership
has made an impact on my life.

We all have critical stages in our lives. I feel sorry for those who feel that they have no choices. Hopefully they follow a trusted family member or friend who will lead them in the right direction. Erik Erikson was one of my favorite theorists because he believed that developing human beings are defined by the choices they make through critical stages of their lives. One of my favorite assignments for future educators was to have them create a timeline of the critical stages in their lives to help them understand the stages promoted by theorists such as Erikson. I wanted them to see how their lives were shaped, to understand that their students also face difficult stages in their life. As thinking human beings, we have many choices that shape the direction of our lives.

Carol Swain implores the American people to choose wisely in her book *Be the People*. She believes that our country is in a critical stage. She shares in the first chapter, "America's foundation is shifting. It is time to think clearly. Who have we been historically, and what kind of nation are we becoming?"[2] She concludes in the last chapter, "Our love for God, our families, future generations— for all who will be required to give an account to God—demands that we take seriously our obligation to warn society of God's impending judgement on those who continue to pursue an ungodly course."[3] Choose well. Swain shares three tasks for Christians in these tumultuous times. First, focus on a personal relationship with God. Second, strengthen your families and churches. Third, help inform, educate, and enlighten others.

We must be well-informed to make good choices. In the first chapter of Proverbs, Solomon implores his son to seek wisdom. "The fear of the Lord is the beginning of knowledge, but fools despise wisdom and instruction" (Proverbs 1:7). Choosing to follow God, the Good Shepherd, will guide us in the right direction. We choose God mostly because of His love for us; He created us and cares for us.

> For God did not send His Son into the world to condemn the world, but that the world through Him might be saved. He who believes in Him is not condemned, but he who does not believe is condemned already, because he has not believed

---

[2] Swain, Carol M. *Be the People* (Nashville, TN: Thomas Nelson, 2011), 17.
[3] Swain, Carol M. *Be the People* (Nashville, TN: Thomas Nelson, 2011), 230.

in the name of the only begotten Son of God. And this is the condemnation, that the light has come into the world, and men loved darkness rather than light, because their deeds were evil. (John 3:17–19)

Whom will you choose? The kingdom of God is at hand. Although people joke about doomsday prophets, John the Baptist was urgent in his call for repentance and baptism. We may not know when the end is coming, but our own death on earth is certain. No one knows when their own day of reckoning will be. Jesus calls for you to follow. Our salvation is a choice to accept eternal life through obedience to Jesus Christ as Lord or following the ways of the world that lead to eternal damnation—wailing and gnashing of teeth. I pray that you do not choose the dark ways of the world but follow the narrow path that leads to eternal life.

– ல –

Key Bible Verses: Joshua 24:15, Matthew 6:24, 2 Peter 1:4–13

Keywords: Eternal, follow(ed), hear, kingdom, master(s), see, serve

Song: "Seek Ye First the Kingdom of God"

Old Testament Command: "I am the Lord your God, who brought you out of the land of Egypt, out of the house of bondage. You shall have no other gods before Me" (Exodus 20:2–3).

Questions:

1. Have you ever been in a situation where you felt as if you had no choices?

2. In a typical day, what directs your path: the laws of this world or the commands of God?

3. What is one allure of the world that you could deny from this day forward, and what practice could you add to be more obedient to the true King of this world and more importantly the next?

Ponderable:

There are many Christian denominations and nondenominations. Does it matter to which one we belong? Mark 9:38–41 says, "Teacher, we saw someone who does not follow us casting out demons in Your name, and we forbade him … But Jesus said, 'Do not forbid him, for no one who works a miracle in My name can soon afterward speak evil of Me. For he who is not against us is on our side.'"

CHAPTER 3

Give All Glory to God

But the hour is coming, and now is, when the true worshippers will worship the Father in spirit and truth; for the Father is seeking such to worship Him.

—John 4:23

The trouble with most of us is that we would rather be ruined by praise than saved by criticism.

—Norman Vincent Peale, *The Power of Positive Thinking*

Church in Berlin, Germany

Worship belongs to God alone, and true worshippers choose to worship Him alone. I have noticed from my Bible readings that angels corrected people who tried to worship them, as in Revelation 19:10: "And I fell at his feet to worship him. But he said to me, 'See that you do not do that! I am your fellow servant, and of your brethren who have the testimony of Jesus. Worship God!'" Worship of anyone or anything other than God is wrong. Jesus' miracles often led to worship of God, not Jesus the Son of Man. For example, Mark 2:12 states after the healing of the paralytic they "glorified God," not Jesus. Likewise, in Luke 5:25–26, both the paralytic and the crowd gave glory to God. If Jesus saw that all glory went to God the Father, then how much more should we give glory to God and not ourselves or others for all miracles great and small? On the other hand, note that worship was accepted after the resurrection, as in Matthew 28:17: "When they saw Him, they worshipped Him."

Whenever we start to believe that we have made a difference or did something praiseworthy, we need to remind ourselves that God is in control. We will not be able to do truly great things until we realize that all good things are actually God's work in our lives. I was blessed to visit a few of the many beautiful churches in Europe. One particular church in Berlin, the Kaiser Wilhelm Memorial Church, was left in its bombed state as a reminder of the destructive nature of wars caused by human sinfulness. Even our most beautiful churches, built for the glory of God, cannot escape the evil actions of humankind.

Men should not accept glory, for all glory and praise belong to God. We sometimes think too highly of ourselves and our actions. Remember the banquet in Luke 14. One should not take the seat of honor, for someone more important may arrive. Proverbs 25:6–7 reinforces this sentiment, "Do not exalt yourself in the presence of the king, and do not stand in the place of great; for it is better that he says to you, 'Come up here,' than that you should be put lower in the presence of the prince, whom your eyes have seen." Give glory for all good things to God.

At this point, I must share one action of churchgoers that irritates me. I have noticed that congregations have increasingly resorted to clapping in church. This often happens after a good song or inspiring message. I want to believe that the members are clapping because they were moved spiritually, but I cannot help but view this as people receiving the praise of men rather than handing over all glory to God. On a few occasions, the preacher has reminded the congregation that the applause belongs to God, not himself. I really appreciate those few comments. Music and preaching should be done to give glory to God, not humans. I sometimes feel as if I am the only one in church who is not clapping, but I hope I am not the only one who knows that all good things come from God, not humans.

I admire those Christian athletes and stars who acknowledge God first when they receive human accolades. God does not need our praise, but we need to praise Him. As a teacher, we are taught the power of expectations. If we live a life where we expect good things to come from God, then we will be more likely to see the good that God provides for us. All good things come from God, not of our own doing but in spite of them. It is a secure feeling when we realize that God will take care of us and allow ourselves to become the person that God desires of us. That is the ultimate power of positive expectations.

Not only should we give God all glory, but we should also accept that we are in need of help. Norman Vincent Peale stated that we can improve with criticism but are ruined by praise. Do we rely on our own devices or recognize that our true help comes from the Lord. "A man's steps are of the Lord; how then can a man understand his own way?" (Proverbs 20:24).

All honor and glory belong to God.

Give unto the LORD, O you mighty ones, give unto the LORD glory and strength. Give unto the LORD the glory due to His name; worship the LORD in the beauty of holiness. The voice of the LORD is over the waters; the God of glory thunders; the LORD is over many waters. The voice of the LORD is powerful; the voice of the LORD is full of majesty. The voice of the LORD breaks the cedars, yes, the LORD splinters the cedars of Lebanon. He makes them also skip like a calf, Lebanon and Sirion like a young wild ox. The voice of the LORD divides the flames of fire. The voice of the LORD shakes the wilderness; the LORD shakes the Wilderness of Kadesh. The voice of the LORD makes the deer give birth, and strips the forests bare; and in His temple everyone says, 'Glory!' The LORD sat enthroned at the Flood, and the LORD sits as King forever. The LORD will give strength to His people; the LORD will bless His people with peace. (Psalm 29:1–11)

Key Bible Verses: 1 Samuel 5:2–4, Mark 2:12, Hebrews 5:5

Keywords: Good, glorify (glorified), glory, worship(ed)(ing)

Song: "O Come, Let Us Adore Him"

Old Testament command: "You shall not make for yourself a carved image—any likeness of anything that is in heaven above, or that is in the earth beneath, or that is in the water under the earth; you shall not bow down to them nor serve them. For I, the LORD your God, am a jealous God, visiting the iniquity of the fathers upon the children to the third and fourth generations of those who hate Me, but showing mercy to thousands, to those who love Me and keep My commandments" (Exodus 20:4–6).

Questions:

1. We need to be careful not to have false idols in our lives. What possessions are you most proud of and why?

2. Is the sanctuary where you worship in better condition (structurally and aesthetically) than your house?

3. How much time do you devote to God each week? Consider your social media postings and consider what it says about your priorities.

Ponderable:

Should where and how we worship change with cultural norms?

The woman said to Him, "Sir, I perceive that You are a prophet. Our fathers worshiped on this mountain, and you Jews say that in Jerusalem is the place where one ought to worship." Jesus said to her, "Woman, believe Me, the hour is coming when you will neither on this mountain, nor in Jerusalem, worship the Father. You worship what you do not know; we know what we worship, for salvation is of the Jews. But the hour is coming, and now is, when the true worshipers will worship the Father in spirit and truth; for the Father is seeking such to worship Him. God is Spirit, and those who worship Him must worship in spirit and truth." (John 4:19–24)

CHAPTER 4

Revere the Names of God

"Father, glorify Your name." Then a voice came from heaven, saying, "I have both glorified it and will glorify it again."

—John 12:28

What's in a name? That which we call a rose by any other name would smell as sweet.

—Shakespeare's *Romeo and Juliet*

Words have meaning and names have power.

—Source unknown

People in power know the power of names and words. The naming of a person, product, or action can affect the perception and reaction of others in sometimes-critical ways. Shakespeare is right that the rose would smell the same, but he is wrong when you consider that a rose may be a big seller or just another rose depending on its name. Advertisers and authors know that words matter. So it is no wonder that Jesus' name was carefully chosen, as were the names of many other prophets in the Bible.

As I did this research, I found it interesting that the name to be given to Jesus, Emmanuel in Matthew 1:23, was only used once in all four gospels. This name appeared only twice in the Old Testament, Isaiah 7:14 and 8:8, so that the name being "God with us" would be fulfilled. It is interesting that God has so many different names in the Bible: Son of God, Son of Man, Teacher, Master, Jesus, which means Savior, Christ, which means the anointed one, Rabbi, and many more. I have heard that scribes had special rules, especially when recording the name of God. Ever since hearing that, I pause before writing any of the many names of God. And it does irritate me whenever any reference to God is not capitalized. There are many hymns that do not have references to God as He or Him with capital letters. I have even noticed it in some versions of the Bible.

Some have said that the sweetest sound one can hear is the sound of one's own name. I know that when I see or hear my name, it gets my attention. I may notice more often than most since my name is so unusual, but there are a few spots in the world that include the name Mara, so I take a picture of the spots when I can. As I have gotten older, I have also adopted the name of "mom" and now "grammy," so, along with many other women in a store, I turn when someone yells, "Mom!" I even look when I know my own children are miles away. My name does get my attention, and the misuse or mispronunciation of a name can be an irritant.

As a teacher, I recognized the value of a name. I worked very hard to learn the names of my high school students early in the year. It was a challenge for me. I also appreciate the work that other teachers put forth, especially the first-grade teacher of my oldest grandchild. She called our house the week before school to make sure that she would pronounce her name correctly. I wish all of my teachers and friends worked that hard. I still hear my name mispronounced by those I encounter.

Sometimes we receive or take on new names as situations, responsibilities, or characteristics change. Many stars and athletes acquire names by choice or accomplishment. You might know Hammerin' Hank, Ali, or the Man in Black. Dave (honey) was also given a name in high school due to his competitive play on the golf team, "Clutch." I must say that I was very proud last year when I officially received the title of doctor when I earned my PhD. However, I am looking forward even more to the new name I will receive when I am able to enter the pearly gates of heaven.

Early in our courtship, my husband and I realized that we rarely used each other's name in conversation, unless we were introducing the other to a friend. Honey was one of our favorite pet names, but we did have several others that we tried. I have recently shared with my grandchildren that sometimes my guardian angel's name is Paw Paw. He is very protective of the ones he loves. Early in our relationship, we devised a coded system to let the other know if something was wrong. It was very simple, actually. We would use our middle names while addressing the other. So instead of asking for Dave or David, I would ask for David Arthur. Or if he asked who was calling, I would say Mara Jane and not Mara. The use of a middle name was a code for "something is wrong." We never had to use it, but it was another testimony to the power that is in a name.

Just as our names are powerful attention-getters, they can also become painful weapons that demonstrate disrespect. Mispronunciation, misuse, and distortion of names are expressions of teasing at best and bullying at its worst. I have noticed that the media has increasingly shown disrespect for the name of God. It has gotten gradually worse throughout my life. I remember as a child that my mother was very upset when I used euphemisms of His name that were commonly used words of expression. Then, as a mother myself, I remember telling my own children to never use His name unless you really are talking to or about Him. It is sad how often I hear His name on television when it is clear that it is only a hollow expression.

"The name of the Lord is a strong tower; the righteous run to it and are safe" (Proverbs 18:10). And Psalm 8:1–9 states,

> O Lord, our Lord, how excellent is Your name in
> all the earth, who have set Your glory above the

heavens! Out of the mouth of babes and nursing infants You have ordained strength, because of Your enemies, that You may silence the enemy and the avenger. When I consider Your heavens, the work of Your fingers, the moon and the stars, which You have ordained, what is man that You are mindful of him, and the son of man that You visit him? For You have made him a little lower than the angels, and You have crowned him with glory and honor. You have made him to have dominion over the works of Your hands; You have put all things under his feet, all sheep and oxen—even the beasts of the field, the birds of the air, and the fish of the sea that pass through the paths of the seas. O Lord, our Lord, how excellent is Your name in all the earth!

Key Bible Verses: Job 1:21 and 2:9, Matthew 1:19, Philippians 2:9

Emmanuel in Matthew 1:23 and Immanuel in Isaiah 7:14 and 8:8

New names given in Revelation 2:17 and 19:12

Keyword: Name

Song: "Precious Name"

Old Testament Command: "You shall not take the name of the Lord your God in vain, for the Lord will not hold him guiltless who takes His name in vain" (Exodus 20:7).

Questions:

1. If you were to name the next baby born in your family, what name would you choose?

2. What name do you prefer to go by? How does it feel when the wrong name is used?

3. What name do you prefer to use when talking to and praying to God? Do you respect all of His names? How serious is cussing/cursing as a sin?

Ponderable:

Should we all have a new name when we give our life to Jesus, as was done for many in scripture? "Simon, to whom He gave the name Peter" (Mark 3:16).

CHAPTER 5

Honor the Natural Order of Creation

For the Son of Man is Lord even of the Sabbath.
—Matthew 12:8

Run your business in harmony with God's laws. This will keep you on an ethical footing. Seek to please God in everything you do.
—David Green of Hobby Lobby

I love to view the natural beauty of calm waters and colorful skies. I considered adding one of my favorite sunset pictures, but no picture can match the beauty of the real thing. One reason I love to see a beautiful sky is the reminder that God is in control; He is our Creator God. People will never be able to predict the weather with certainty. That is comforting for me. I consider the weather to be a hug from God, because He has never left me in bad weather. In fact, I gave a sermon about miracles one Sunday that described the weather as a minor miracle. I cannot count the number of times that a rain stayed calm until after I entered the building, and then the heavy downpour arrived.

While we live on earth, we are frail and need rest. From the very beginning, as shared in Genesis, our Creator instituted a day of rest.

We need rest because we are human and need time to refresh our bodies. However, in heaven we will have eternal life and strength. The Sabbath is a gift for us, not a burden. It is a reminder that as long as we remain in our human bodies, we will have human weaknesses. It is yet one more reason to look forward to the day when we can enter our eternal home.

Jesus did many things while on earth as an example for us. He rested. He prayed. He was even baptized by John the Baptist as a visible example of how we should live. His actions as the Son of Man were done for our own edification to help us know how to live. I often wonder what God would think about the world today. Is our civilized world too far apart from the created world? Should we attempt to return to the garden of Eden and reject the many so-called civilized gadgets of this world? I do know that we can never have a perfect world while on earth, but that should not stop us from trying to make this world as close to God's intended creation as possible. I cannot help but wonder if our advanced civilization is really not advanced at all. Perhaps we could learn a lesson from the Tower of Babel and move away from our so-called advances.

In addition to living more organically, we should remember that our body is a temple for the indwelling of the Holy Spirit. We should not take in what is not beneficial, like tobacco, drugs, unwanted chemicals, or pornography, but we should also avoid excesses of food, drugs, etc. The following from Proverbs is a harsh reminder to be careful with this temple we refer to as our body. "When you sit down to eat with a ruler, consider carefully what is before you; and put a knife to your throat if you are a man given to appetite. Do not desire his delicacies, for they are deceptive food. Do not overwork to be rich; because of your own understanding, cease!" (Proverbs 23:1–4). It is not easy to refuse the riches when offered, but we should use the prophet Daniel as an example of the goodness to come when we obey our Creator.

Living in harmony with creation is a worthy goal, as shared above by David Green. We must honor God by honoring creation and the way God created us. We were made for a reason. Psalm 19 states well how creation is a revelation of the beautiful things God has in store for us:

> The heavens declare the glory of God; and the firmament shows His handiwork. Day unto day utters speech, and night unto night reveals knowledge. There is no speech nor language where their voice is not heard. Their line has gone out through all the earth, and their words to the end of the world. In them He has set a tabernacle for the sun, which is like a bridegroom coming out of his chamber, and rejoices like a strong man to run its race. Its rising is from one end of heaven, and its circuit to the other ends; and there is nothing hidden from its heat. The law of the Lord is perfect, converting the soul; the testimony of the Lord is sure, making wise the simple; the statutes of the Lord are right, rejoicing the heart; the commandment of the Lord is pure, enlightening the eyes; the fear of the Lord is clean, enduring forever; the judgments of the Lord are true and righteous altogether. More to be desired are they than gold, yea, than much fine gold; sweeter also than honey and the honeycomb. Moreover by them Your servant is warned, and in keeping them there is great reward. Who can understand his errors? Cleanse me from secret faults. Keep back Your servant also from presumptuous sins; let them not have dominion over me. Then I shall be blameless, and I shall be innocent of great transgression. Let the words of my mouth and the meditation of my heart be acceptable in Your sight, O Lord, my strength and my Redeemer.

As you may have noticed, the Psalms and Proverbs are used in conjunction with most of the commands. The Old Testament has valuable knowledge for us as a basis for righteous living. However, the New Testament was necessary to fulfill the prophecy and complete the knowledge needed to be saved. Each one of my commandments matches an Old Testament command but is modified to align with Jesus' perfect desires for us. The Old Testament laid a foundation of holy action, and the New Testament urges us to renew our hearts in love toward God and neighbor. These first four commandments of chapters 2 through 5 are about loving God and honoring His creative powers (love the way we were made). Our loyalties should always belong to God foremost. The next six chapters are slightly more secular, sharing how to follow Jesus' example by honoring God's creation in service to others. These chapters are not in the same order as the commands from Exodus for a reason. The next three should be a reflection of how we should live because of God's influence on our lives, and the final three relate more specifically to actions that more directly affect others around us. The final two chapters are added to conclude the commands of the gospels.

Key Bible Verses: Isaiah 58:13–14, Exodus 16:29, Luke 6:5, Colossians 2:16

Keywords: Ask, fast, honor, pray, Sabbath, wait, watch

Song: "Take Time to be Holy"

Old Testament Command: "Remember the Sabbath day, to keep it holy. Six days you shall labor and do all your work, but the seventh day is the Sabbath of the Lord your God. In it you shall do no work: you, nor your son, nor your daughter, nor your male servant, nor your female servant, nor your cattle, nor your stranger who is within your gates. For in six days the Lord made the heavens and the earth, the sea, and all that is in them, and rested the seventh day. Therefore the Lord blessed the Sabbath day and hallowed it" (Exodus 20:8–11).

Questions:

1. What is your sleep cycle? Do you need additional rest/naps during the day?

2. What in nature provides you with the most spiritual renewal?

3. What areas in your life are contrary to the original works of creation? (For example, gasoline exhaust is bad for the environment. Chemical engineering, including genetically modified organisms, is not natural for plants used for food.)

Ponderable:

Should we attempt to make this world like the garden of Eden, completely eco-friendly? John 1:1–3 says, "In the beginning was the

Word, and the Word was with God, and the Word was God. He was in the beginning with God. All things were made through Him, and without Him nothing was made that was made." Creation started out good, so with Jesus' sacrifice on the cross, could we return to the good or must we wait for the second coming?

CHAPTER 6

Remain Sexually Pure

Blessed are the pure in heart, for they shall see God.
—Matthew 5:8

The Christian rule is, "Either marriage, with complete faithfulness to your partner, or else total abstinence."

—C.S. Lewis

Churchyard in Mississippi

I married Dave on July 15, 1974, and look forward to many more years together. I was lucky to find a God-fearing man who wanted to attend church every Sunday as a family. We married young and had three terrific children. My children often say that I was born in a bubble. I agree. I was lucky to grow up in an area where I was unaware of divorces and knew no single parents. As far as I knew, every student in my school had a mother and father at home. My family went to church every Sunday. I met my husband in high school, and we married after one year in college. We recently attended the fiftieth wedding anniversary of a dear cousin. I treasure my family memories and feel fondly toward all of my family members. I believe that God intended families to be a support system. God created male and female to help one another. We all have positions in family and life to bring stability and support to God's perfect plan for everyone.

A stable family encourages purity. Proverbs says much about the dangers of sexual impurity and concludes with an entire chapter describing the virtuous woman, the Proverbs 31 Lady. Solomon was a wise man and specifically warns his son of the dangers of adultery in chapters 6 and 7 of Proverbs. "For by means of a harlot, a man is reduced to a crust of bread; and an adulteress will prey upon his precious life. … So is he who goes in to his neighbor's wife; whoever touches her shall not be innocent. … Whoever commits adultery with a woman lacks understanding; he who does so destroys his own soul" (Proverbs 6:26–32). "Do not let your heart turn aside to her ways, do not stray into her paths; for she has cast down many wounded, and all who were slain by her were strong men. Her house is the way to hell, descending to the chambers of death" (Proverbs 7:25–27). The New Testament supports these warnings against sexual impurity. In Romans 1:24–27, foolish and wicked people give into their lusts, dishonoring their created bodies. Jude 1:7 warns against "sexual immorality and going after strange flesh." I will expand upon this in three specific areas: creation, celibacy, and marriage.

First, we were created as sexual beings; God created them as male and female (Genesis 1:27). Jesus restated this in Matthew 19:4, saying, "Have you not read that He who made them at the beginning made them male and female." It seems clear that our sexual bodies are made to be one gender, and any attempt to change that would be due to an abnormality, not normal. This is how homosexuals and transgender people have been perceived for a long time. They are not to be persecuted, but it is not normal. For me, I believe that we must be very wary of doing anything to change what God created as good. We should honor the way we were created rather than taking God's place and trying to change ourselves. Accept your created self and know that God loves you. John Shore[4] referred to Genesis 1:27 and several other verses as clobber verses. I do not condone "clobbering" anyone for their chosen lifestyle, but I think that Christians should in turn be allowed to maintain their own personal beliefs and churches may decide what is considered sin for their congregations. The religious liberty in the United States is a precious thing that should never be taken away.

Some research has been done by Simon LeVay[5]. He has found biological differences among gay persons and hopes for more research to understand the belief that some people are born gay. His research supports the biology of same-sex attractions based on genes, sex hormones, and interactions with the developing brain. John Shore argues that people who are made differently should not be treated unfairly, especially by Christians who profess that God is love. I certainly agree that all those who treat others with hatred are wrong. Judgement belongs to God, not humans, for we have all fallen short of perfection. Even the one good enough to judge others treated others with compassion, not ignoring their sin but telling them, "Go and sin no more" (John 8:11).

Second, celibacy is ignored too often when gender and sexual

---

[4] Shore, John. *Unfair* (Columbia, SC: John Shore, 2013).
[5] LeVay, Simon. *Gay, Straight, and the Reason Why* (Oxford, NY: Oxford University Press, 2017).

orientation are discussed. Jesus, John the Baptist, and Paul were not married; they were all celibate. All three are proof that we can love others very deeply without physical intimacy. Jesus was celibate and believed that our spiritual relationships were much more important than our sexual ones. There are no marriages in heaven.

> Do you not know that your bodies are members of Christ? Shall I then take the members of Christ and make them members of a harlot? Certainly not! Or do you not know that he who is joined to a harlot is one body with her? For "the two," He says, "shall become one flesh." But he who is joined to the Lord is one spirit with Him. Flee sexual immorality. Every sin that a man does is outside the body, but he who commits sexual immorality sins against his own body. (1 Corinthians 6:15–18)

Paul exhorts his followers to stay celibate if possible to "glorify God in your body" (1 Corinthians 6:20) and that "it is good for a man not to touch a woman" (1 Corinthians 7:1), but "because of sexual immorality, let each man have his own wife" (1 Corinthians 7:2). In the gospel of Matthew, Jesus was questioned about divorce laws.

> His disciples said to Him, "If such is the case of the man with his wife, it is better not to marry." But He said to them, "All cannot accept this saying, but only those to whom it has been given: for there are eunuchs who were born thus from their mother's womb, and there are eunuchs who were made eunuchs by men, and there are eunuchs who have made themselves eunuchs for the kingdom of heaven's sake. He who is able to accept it, let him accept it." (Matthew 19:10–12)

The celibate lifestyle is one that should be included in sex education and gender lifestyle discussions. It is too often ignored, especially in this sex-driven world.

Wise people control their fleshly desires, which makes me wonder why society is becoming more and more unwise. Hollywood produces many movies with ratings that warn of sexual content and very few movies rated for general audiences. Either they do not want to make family-friendly movies or they believe that sex in movies is the easy way to sell them. I believe that Hollywood promotes sex as a false idol. At this point I must interject how much I admire Vice President Mike Pence's relationship with his wife. He understands the problem of proximity and never has business lunches alone with another female. The main street media does not understand the wisdom of this, but as a frail and envious woman—I understand.

Follow C.S. Lewis's rule, "Either marriage, with complete faithfulness to your partner, or else total abstinence."[6] Sexual purity means celibacy or monogamous marriage. Marriage is for life. Families are originated in marriage. God uses earthly marriage as an image of the love between Jesus and the church. Jesus is the bridegroom, and the church is the bride.

> Let us be glad and rejoice and give Him glory, for the marriage of the Lamb has come, and His wife has made herself ready. And to her it was granted to be arrayed in fine linen, clean and bright, for the fine linen is the righteous acts of the saints. Then he said to me, "Write: Blessed are those who are called to the marriage supper of the Lamb!" And he said to me, "These are the true sayings of God." (Revelation 19:7–9)

Third, marriages were instituted to form families. Jesus was born into a loving family, and His first miracle was at a wedding

---

[6] Lewis, C. S. *Mere Christianity* (Westwood, NJ: Barbour and Company, 1952).

celebration. "This beginning of signs Jesus did in Cana of Galilee, and manifested His glory; and His disciples believed in Him" (John 2:11). The miracle was initiated by Jesus' mother. Jesus had one mother and one father. God created males and females. The ideal marriage is between one man and one woman. The two shall become one, and no one should come between them. Jesus did not condemn those who were divorced but acknowledged divorce as an imperfection and commanded them to go and sin no more. I believe that Jesus would agree with C. S. Lewis in proclaiming that a sexual union should only happen within the confines of marriage and only with the marital partner. Although some men in the Old Testament had multiple wives, this is not present in the New Testament. Two, not three or more, will become one.

Further, Jesus used the symbolism of marriage to represent the love that God has for the church and likewise that the church should have for God. The true love in a marriage is not the physical intimacy but the spiritual union. Jesus called Himself a bridegroom. "As long as they have the bridegroom with them they cannot fast" (Mark 2:19). "Can the friends of the bridegroom mourn as long as the bridegroom is with them?" (Matthew 9:15). In the final book of the Bible, "And the Spirit and the bride say, 'Come!'" (Revelation 22:17). The love that God wants us to experience is not the physical pleasures of the flesh but the spiritual love that lasts forever and ever in heaven.

Our bodies are holy temples, holy vessels. We should control our worldly desires to honor the Holy Spirit that dwells within us. We honor our Creator and bless those around us by treating our bodies with holy reverence. Just as discussed in chapter 5, creation was good. We should follow the natural order of creation established by our Creator. And as shared in chapter 2, we should choose the goodness of our positions in family and life.

Blessed is every one who fears the Lord, who walks in His ways. When you eat the labor of your hands, you shall be happy, and it shall be well with you. Your wife shall be like a fruitful vine in the very heart of your house, your children like olive plants all around your table. Behold, thus shall the man be blessed who fears the Lord. The Lord bless you out of Zion, and may you see the good of Jerusalem all the days of your life. Yes, may you see your children's children. Peace be upon Israel. (Psalm 128:1–6)

– ☙ –

Key Bible Verses: Proverbs 5:15–23, John 2:1–11, Matthew 5:27–28, Mark 10:2–9, 1 Corinthians 6:15–20, 7:7–9, 1 Peter 2:9–12

Keywords: Body, bridegroom, flesh, holy, temple

Song: "Take My Life and Let it Be Consecrated Lord to Thee"

Old Testament command: "You shall not commit adultery" (Exodus 20:14)

Questions:

1. In what ways does society encourage immoral behavior?

2. What is one initiative that would encourage our culture to be more moral?

3. If we were to develop a sexual education course for middle school children, what would be included? For high school? For elementary students?

Ponderable:

But He said to them, "All cannot accept this saying, but only those to whom it has been given: for there are eunuchs who were born thus from their mother's womb, and there are eunuchs who were made eunuchs by men, and there are eunuchs who have made themselves eunuchs for the kingdom of heaven's sake. He who is able to accept it, let him accept it." (Matthew 19:11–12)

CHAPTER 7

Honor Your Family

Then He went down with them and came to Nazareth, and was subject to them, but His mother kept all these things in her heart.

—Luke 2:51

No society can long sustain itself unless its members have learned the sensitivities, motivations and skills involved in assisting and caring for other human beings.

—Urie Bronfenbrenner

Family at birthday party

Just as we should revere the name of our Creator, we should also give honor to our family name by giving family members respect for their love and support. Families are the first introduction to methods of love, support, and fellowship with all people. I used a quote from Urie Bronfenbrenner above because of his theory that stresses the value of human relationships, which start ultimately with the immediate family. His ecological theory describes a system of interrelationships that affect the growing child. His work in this area at Cornell University led him to be a cofounder of the national Head Start program in 1965, a part of LBJ's war on poverty. Relationships matter, and our relationships begin with our family.

The family in which Jesus was born was well documented in the gospels, and His life on earth affected the world so dramatically that the calendar dates changed to using BC and AD. We do not have a full biography of His early years, but we do know that Mary held a special place in her heart for her child, just as all parents should. "And the Child grew and became strong in spirit, filled with wisdom; and the grace of God was upon Him" (Luke 2:40). We also know that Jesus was obedient and took His Jewish heritage seriously. He felt comfortable in the temple discussing the religious topics of His day. At the age of twelve, He was in the temple in Jerusalem, "sitting in the midst of the teachers, both listening to them and asking them questions. And all who heard Him were astonished at His understanding and answers" (Luke 2:46–47). If I could have one wish, it would be that all children could have two parents, a loving home, and a decent household income. Parenthood is not easy, and I relied on Dave many times as the head of the house to provide leadership, security, and Christian love. God's plan was for a child to be born to a man and woman, but also into a family. Our lives affect many generations to come. The Bible shares the generations that came before Jesus because family does matter. The genealogies of Jesus are shared in both Matthew 1 and Luke 3.

After the story of Jesus in the temple at age twelve, we do not have any more knowledge of Joseph as Jesus' earthly father. When

Jesus begins His ministry, all references to His Father are of God. Jesus was the Son of Man or humankind and the Son of God the Father. His human origins were only important to the Jewish faith in that He was born into the house of David to fulfill the prophets. It is of note that Father is used 244 times in the gospels, with only a few references to His earthly father, Joseph.

Families should be respected. Proverbs shares much about the role of families in our lives.

> My son, hear the instruction of your father, and do not forsake the law of thy mother; for they will be a graceful ornament on your head, and chains about your neck. (Proverbs 1:8–9)

> My son, do not despise the chastening of the Lord, nor detest His correction; for whom the Lord loves He corrects, just as a father the son in whom he delights. (Proverbs 3:11–12)

> Hear, my children, the instruction of a father, and give attention to know understanding; for I give you good doctrine: do not forsake my law. When I was my father's son, tender and the only one in the sight of my mother, he also taught me, and said unto me: "Let your heart retain my words; keep my commands, and live." (Proverbs 4:1–4)

In a perfect world, we would all have a holy mother and father to love us and teach us God's ways. Unfortunately, this is not the case for all children. Further, God may not want us to remain with our family but to branch out and share Christian fellowship with others. Jesus moved out of the house and developed a new familial relationship with His followers, especially the twelve chosen apostles. At one point, He shared some very difficult statements about family.

Do you suppose that I came to give peace on earth? I tell you, not at all, but rather division. For from now on five in one house will be divided: three against two, and two against three. Father will be divided against son and son against father, mother against daughter and daughter against mother, mother-in-law against her daughter-in-law and daughter-in-law against her mother-in-law. (Luke 12:51–53)

It was God's perfect plan for us to grow up in a loving Christian home. However, we should not get too comfortable. We must branch out and find more brothers and sisters in Christ to fellowship with and follow in obedience to God's plan for our lives. I feel fortunate to have both a loving family and some special groups to assist me in my desire to follow Christ. Above, I have pictured a grouping of my immediate family from a recent milestone birthday. I was blessed with three children, two brothers, and three sisters. I treasure the times that I am able to be with all of my siblings, for the six of us are not together as often as I would like. Other special groups include my church family, the Daughters of the American Revolution (DAR), and Kappa Delta Pi (KDP, an international honor society for educators). Family groups are not always related by blood but always have an obvious closeness due to shared beliefs or goals.

Why can't we all just get along? It is a hard saying that Jesus came to divide. Also, it is difficult when He did not immediately respond to His mother and brothers, but stated that His family was anyone who followed the commands of God. However, could we not respect our own families and the families of others? Just as we should give respect to the names of God, perhaps we should also respect our family groups. And perhaps we should respect other people's families as we would want them to respect our own.

Relationships matter. In many of the writings in education and beyond, the value of relationships is increasingly highlighted.

For example, a recent book by Krznaric[7] about living starts with nurturing relationships. The families in which we belong by both birth and by choice have an amazing effect on our lives. It has been said that the single most important choice that we make for our future success is the lifelong partner that we choose. This is the person who determines the family that we will have for the rest of our lives.

– ❧ –

---

[7] Krznaric, Roman. *How Should We Live?* (Katonah, NY: BlueBridge, 2011).

Key Bible Verses: Isaiah 62:5, Matthew 9:15, Revelation 18:23, 21:9, 22:17

Keywords: Chosen, father, mother

Song: "Just As I Am"

Old Testament command: "Honor your father and your mother, that your days may be long upon the land which the Lord your God is giving you" (Exodus 20:12).

Questions:

1. If an outsider were to study your parents and how you were raised, what would they say your future family and career would be (destiny based on nurture)? How well does it match your actual life?

2. What is the most common cause of family dysfunction? What should be the response for Christians?

3. Who are members of your family? Are they all related by blood? Do they all share God's will for your life?

Ponderable:

Since Mary had other sons to watch after her, why did Jesus say the following (Matthew 12:46–50)" "When Jesus therefore saw His mother, and the disciple whom He loved standing by, He said to his mother, 'Woman, behold your son!' Then He said to the disciple, 'Behold your mother!' And from that hour that disciple took her to his own home" (John 19:26–27).

Chapter 8

Be Humble and Obedient

As the living Father sent Me, and I live because of
the Father, so he who feeds on Me will live because
of Me. This is the bread which came down from
heaven—not as your fathers ate the manna, and are
dead. He who eats this bread will live forever.

—John 6:57–58

Power corrupts and absolute power corrupts
absolutely.

—Lord Acton

The devil tempted Adam and Eve to sin with a promise that they
would "be like God" (Genesis 3:5). Power is tempting for people, and
they should not possess too much, as the quote above suggests. Lord
Acton was a nineteenth-century historian and lover of individual
liberty. He appreciated the freedom and liberty of the United States
and was wary of any large concentration of power. His sentiments
match those in Proverbs:

How much better to get wisdom than gold! And to
get understanding is to be chosen rather than silver.
The highway of the upright is to depart from evil;

he who keeps his way preserves his soul. Pride goes before destruction, and a haughty spirit before a fall. Better to be of a humble spirit with the lowly, than to divide the spoil with the proud. He who heeds the word wisely will find good, and whoever trusts in the Lord, happy is he. (Proverbs 16:16–20)

People are corrupted by power, as history has repeatedly shown. All power rightfully belongs to God, and even Jesus accepted His position on earth with humility when tried by the Sanhedrin and Pilate. "Pilate therefore said to Him, 'Are You a king then?' Jesus answered, 'You say rightly that I am a king. For this cause I was born, and for this cause I have come into the world, that I should bear witness to the truth. Everyone who is of the truth hears My voice'" (John 18:37). We should accept our reason for which we were born. God made us and has a perfect plan for our lives. It is our job to accept our position and remain obedient to His commands. It is not wrong to work hard and improve your station in life, but always be content with your current station. The alternative to contentment and acceptance is envy that eats away at inner peace. How many are envious of power and try to grab it, only to end up in utter destruction in the end? We all have envied someone who seemed to have more than ourselves. I remember as a child watching others win first place, and I always felt as if I could never win. I was often in second place but never first. I could not even win the spot of shortest student in my classroom; there was one student shorter as we lined up for special events.

It is not always easy to accept ourselves as God created us. But God made everything, and it was good in every way, as shared in chapter 5. Rather than being envious of others, we need to search out God's plan for our lives. It may not be obvious to us right away, but we must accept it with obedience and faith. Sometimes we may feel powerless in our current circumstances, but God does have a plan. Remember Joseph; it must have been miserable to be sold into slavery by his own brothers and then sent to prison because of a false accusation. However, Joseph was obedient and immensely patient. As a result, he became the most powerful man in Egypt next to Pharaoh. God has a special plan for each one of us. Be patient and obedient. Choose obedience; this is the bread of life that will nourish us to be ready to do God's will for our lives. Do not worry. God has everything under control.

God has a plan for you. You might not be the head, but you will have an important part in the body of Christ. God's creation is good, and He has given each of us different talents. Do not be like the unwise servant who hid his talents and was chided as a "wicked and lazy servant" (Matthew 25:26). In Jesus' time, there were many disciples but only twelve chosen apostles. These special twelve were ordained with specific powers for teaching, preaching, healing, and miracle making. You may not have the power to forgive sins, but you have God's power available if needed to do God's will. Do not underestimate the power of your Lord and Savior. Ask anything and it will be done in accordance with God's perfect plan. Remember, even Jesus was unwilling to test God during His temptations in the desert, but He was able to perform many miracles to further the kingdom's goals.

I have entered retirement but am still unsure of my purpose. Have I missed opportunities to turn others toward God? Have I done some good works unawares? I remember when I decided to become a teacher. It was not easy because I had a career that paid fairly well. My own son accused me of lowering our family's standard of living. I prayed a lot before changing careers. I remembered praying for my future students, hoping that I could make a difference for them. I knew I could help them understand mathematics. I was hoping that I could help them live a better life. I also remember thinking that I might not ever know the good that I might do for another, but I needed to do it anyway.

Jesus understood the position God gave Him.

And He was handed the book of the prophet Isaiah. And when He had opened the book, He found the place where it was written: "The Spirit of the Lord is upon Me, because He has anointed Me to preach the gospel to the poor; He has sent Me to heal the brokenhearted, to proclaim liberty to the captives and recovery of sight to the blind, to set at liberty those who are oppressed; to proclaim the acceptable year of the Lord." Then He closed the book, and gave it back to the attendant and sat down. And the eyes of all who were in the synagogue were fixed on Him. And He began to say to them, "Today this scripture is fulfilled in your hearing." (Luke 4:17–21)

Accept your position in life, your strengths and weaknesses, and partake of your daily bread or manna through obedience to God's commands. Our manna from heaven is always enough; be content. Be willing to swallow your pride, eat humble pie, and never put more on your plate than you can handle. Eat your daily bread of obedience to God in whatever position in life you hold. You may never know all the good you do for others in this life, but do it anyway. If you can do something for God to further the kingdom, just do it with acceptance and obedience in faith.

– ଛ –

Key Bible Verses: Esther 9:26–32, John 14:26–27, Philippians 4:4–9

Keywords: Authority, baptize(ed)(ing), peace, power, repent, reward

Song: "God Will Take Care of You"

Old Testament Command: "You shall not covet your neighbor's house; you shall not covet your neighbor's wife, nor his male servant, nor his female servant, nor his ox, nor his donkey, nor anything that is your neighbor's" (Exodus 20:17).

Questions

1. If one person in the world were to be given superpowers from God, who do you think that should be?

2. In what situations do you have more power or less power than you feel you deserve? Are there any situations in which you feel helpless, with no power or choices?

3. If you had the power to do one thing for the world, what would you do?

Ponderable:

Why did Jesus so often ask others to keep quiet about His miraculous powers? After the glorious transfiguration, "Now as they came down from the mountain, Jesus commanded them, saying, 'Tell the vision to no one until the Son of Man is risen from the dead" (Matthew 17:9). After healing a leper, He "charged him to tell no one" (Luke 5:14). If the miracles were proof of His saving power, why would He display the power and then want it hidden?

CHAPTER 9

Give with Compassion

Give us day by day our daily bread.

—Luke 11:3

You can have everything in life that you want if you will just help enough other people get what they want.

—Zig Ziglar

Be kind, for everyone you meet is fighting a harder battle.

—Plato

Making a book donation

Participation in Wreaths Across America

The command to refrain from stealing seems so obvious to any adult who wants to live in harmony with his or her neighbors. But giving is challenging, especially when we have a limited supply of things to give. Giving with compassion is easier with those who are lovable than with those who are unknown or unkind. Does God really want us to love our enemies? We do not want to be near some people, let alone give them some of our limited resources.

My daughter April has always been kind and compassionate with others (except with her mother during her teen years), and now she is teaching her children to be a Christian "giver" as well. Above are two of my favorite pictures of their giving spirit. They are always happy to assist me, such as when I collected children's books for a school project. They also volunteer to help with groups of their own, such as the Wreaths Across America event. They volunteer their time, collect for worthy causes, and visit those with special needs. When they were making frequent visits to a nursing home, it reminded me of my teen years when my mother made regular visits to a nursing home for her stepmother.

Giving is an outward sign of the Christian love that we should have for all of God's creation. The biggest difference between the Old Testament commandments and the New Testament teachings is the motivation of the follower. The Old Testament stressed actions motivated by doing what was right for an all-powerful God. The New Testament stresses actions motivated by love for both God and others. It reminds me of two current education topics: outcome-based instruction and transformative mind-sets. Just as the Old Testament relied on visible action, teachers realize that it is hard to see inside the mind, so data-based instruction must rely on visible outcomes as evidence of learning. However, the best learning is initiated through intrinsic motivation. Once students can understand and buy into a proper mind-set for learning, then they become self-motivated and ideally regulate their own learning.

Practically speaking, giving must be limited to what we can afford in both money and time. However, God has boundless resources. Does that mean that we have no limits when providing for the multitude of needs of others? Luke 12:23 does say that life is more than meat and the body more than clothing. Can we possibly provide for others' needs so they can become the individuals God desires them to be? When I see someone who is sick, I am not a doctor who could provide healing medicine. When I see someone in a wheelchair, I do not feel capable of a healing miracle for them to walk. When I see a riotous teen, I am afraid to approach them, let alone preach the gospel. Do we limit ourselves too much when it comes to helping others?

I sometimes feel like the rich young ruler when I throw out another mailing request for help. I do not have enough money to help everyone who asks. I do not have the energy or mind-set to stop and help every individual who seems to be incomplete. The rich young ruler walked away because he cared more about his riches than following Jesus. Do I care more about my worldly possessions than fulfilling God's desire to show compassion and assistance to all of His creation? Perhaps I walk away sadly too often.

What should we do to be a cheerful giver for Christ? One good answer for many questions is prayer and fasting. I cannot tell you what you should do, but I can share those things that do work and that I am still working on. In a nutshell, carpe diem. Notice others where they are so you can notice the needs of others. One reason I switched careers to enter the education profession was because of a need that I observed. Too many students disliked a subject that I enjoyed as a student—mathematics. Also, notice your own strengths and continue to learn more/hone your skills. I learned at an early age that I was a good student, especially in mathematics. With the help of my parents, I learned as much as I could both in and outside of school. One of my most treasured paperback books of that time was titled *Fun with Math*. It is probably out of print, but there are many books that encourage logical thinking through games and puzzles. Continue to increase your talents and be aware of the needs of those around you. Seize the many opportunities available to you through chance or more probably divine providence.

God desires for us to use our talents with compassion for others.

> The desire of the righteous is only good, but the expectation of the wicked is wrath. There is one who scatters, yet increases more; and there is one who withholds more than is right, but it leads to poverty. The generous soul will be made rich, and he who waters will also be watered himself. The people will curse him who withholds grain, but blessing will be on the head of him who sells it. He who earnestly seeks good finds favor, but trouble will come to him who seeks evil. (Proverbs 11:23–27)

I am probably held back from sharing with others more because I see my own glass as half empty rather than half full. This is one area where you may test God. He will provide for you even when you over give or perhaps because you over give. "He who gives to the poor will not lack, but he who hides his eyes will have many curses" (Proverbs 28:27).

– ༄ –

Key Bible Verses: Psalm 103:2–4, Matthew 10:1,8, James 5:16

Keywords: Bread, fruit, give, heart, water

Song: "I Surrender All"

Old Testament command: "You shall not steal" (Exodus 20:15).

Questions:

1. What is your favorite charity outside of your church? Think of one way you could help support a charity other than simply donating money.

2. What possessions could you do without? What things would you go back into the fire to save?

3. As Christians, it is hard to say no to anyone in need. But we do have limited resources and would not have enough to live on if we gave to everyone who asked. Should we give to all who ask? How can we be Christians and say *no*?

Ponderable:

Is it possible to be too generous?

But I say to you who hear: love your enemies, do good to those who hate you, bless those who curse you, and pray for those who spitefully use you. To him who strikes you on the one cheek, offer the other also. And from him who takes away your cloak, do not withhold your tunic either. Give to everyone who asks of you. And from him who takes away your goods do not ask them back. And just as you want men should to do to you, you also do to them likewise. (Luke 6:27–31)

CHAPTER 10

Forgive and Heal

Then Jesus said, "Father, forgive them, for they do
not know what they do."

—Luke 23:34

Treat a man as he is and he will remain as he is.
Treat a man as he can and should be and he will
become as he can and should be.

—Stephen R. Covey, *The 7 Habits of Highly
Effective People*

Be helpful, not hurtful. Forgive those who commit evil acts, for
no one was created for evil but only for good. Judas and Peter are
examples of how evil actions do not have to define a person. Both
turned their back on Jesus, but one was forgiven and the other did
not even ask for forgiveness. The Holocaust Memorial in Berlin is a
solemn reminder of the evil actions committed in war. When people
are not able to live in civility together and are unable to forgive
perceived transgressions, atrocities happen. The German people,
especially in Berlin, have many reminders of their past incivilities
so this will never happen again. They want to get along with all the
people of the world and never return to the evil nationalism that
Hitler espoused. "He who despises his neighbor sins; but he who

has mercy on the poor, happy is he. Do they not go astray who devise evil? But mercy and truth belong to those who devise good" (Proverbs 14:21–22).

We should always see people for who they can and should be. I have always done that with my own children. My daughter Tina and I have a special kind of chemistry, and we have always been able to complement one another. I wish I could see everyone in the world with the positive, rose-colored glasses with which I see Tina. We should all look at God's creation for what it was intended to be rather than its current flawed condition. Tina and I have a joke about loving each other's butts. It all started when she realized that I always started my corrections of her behavior with, "Tina, I love you but ___ (fill in the blank)." The world would be a better place if we loved everyone's butts. We often joke about loving each other's butts. I guess she lets me know about her rules now that she is grown. I must live by her rules when I visit her home. For example, "Mom, I love you, but please take your shoes off when you come in the door. I like to keep the floors clean."

However, it is really hard to forgive when one is really hurting. I really admire those who can forgive in the face of personal tragedy. Perhaps you know someone who has forgiven others of heinous acts against a loved one. I am not sure if I could do it; I know that I could only forgive through the grace of God. We should forgive others because God first forgave us. It reminds me of a wonderful sermon given by a former student of mine. In essence, he shared that evil actions are the work of the devil. Blame Satan, not the person. Instead, see that person for the way God created him or her, not by the way that the devil has worked through him or her. Forgive and help him or her become the person that God intended him or her to be.

Further, everyone is in need of some type of healing. We may not need to forgive, but we can help with restorative healing. We must be ethical Christians, and the first rule of ethics is to do no harm. The next step is to heal. It is not our job to judge. Consider the many healings of Jesus; He never condemned them but simply said, "Neither do I condemn you; go and sin no more" (John 8:11). Not all in need of healing have sinned, as shown by the blind man. Jesus said, "Neither this man nor his parents sinned, but that the works of God should be revealed in him" (John 9:3).

I must admit that I do not always recognize the needs of others, but when we do see them, we should act in Christian love. How far should that act of healing go? How much power do we have to heal? These are difficult questions for which everyone must seek answers. Sometimes I get too wrapped up in my own chores and forget to see the needs of others. I am working at looking at others more and reflecting on what, if anything, I can do to help others. I must admit that I have missed some opportunities. Also, I have been the recipient of the kindness of others as well. I must live in the moment and be intentional in my desire to help others whenever I can and as often as I can.

> Bless the Lord, O my soul, and forget not all His benefits: who forgives all your iniquities, who heals all your diseases, who redeems your life from destruction, who crowns you with lovingkindness and tender mercies, who satisfies your mouth with good things, so that your youth is renewed like the eagle's. The Lord executes righteousness and judgment for all who are oppressed. He made known His ways to Moses, His acts to the children of Israel. The Lord is merciful and gracious, slow to anger, and abounding in mercy. He will not always strive with us, nor will He keep His anger forever. He hath not dealt with us according to our sins, nor punished us according to our iniquities. For as the heaven are high above the earth, so great is His mercy toward those who fear Him; as far as the east is from the west, so far has He removed

our transgressions from us. As a father pities his children, so the Lord pities those who fear Him. For He knows our frame; He remembers that we are dust. As for man, his days are like grass; as a flower of the field, so he flourishes. For the wind passes over it, and it is gone, and its place remembers it no more. But the mercy of the Lord is from everlasting to everlasting on those who fear Him, and His righteousness to children's children. (Psalm 103:2–17)

Key Bible Verses: Daniel 9:2–19, Psalm 86:3–7, Matthew 11:4–5, 1 John 1:8–9

Keywords: Forgive, heal(ed), judge, kill

Song: "Amazing Grace"

Old Testament Command: "You shall not murder" (Exodus 20:13).

Questions:

1. What is hardest for you to forgive?

2. Have you ever misjudged someone and later became good friends?

3. Reach out to an enemy today. Pray for him or her and send a note of encouragement. You do not know what battles he or she is facing.

Ponderable:

Should we never fight back?

And He said to them, "When I sent you without money bag, knapsack, and sandals, did you lack anything?" So they said, "Nothing." Then He said to them, "But now, he who has a money bag, let him take it, and likewise a knapsack; and he who has no sword, let him sell his garment and buy one. For I say to you that this which is written must still be accomplished in Me: 'And He was numbered with the transgressors.' For the things concerning Me have an end." So they said, "Lord, look, here are two swords." And He said to them, "It is enough." (Luke 22:35–38)

CHAPTER 11

Speak with Honesty and Truth

Go therefore and make disciples of all nations, baptizing them in the name of the Father and of the Son and of the Holy Spirit.

—Matthew 28:19

Say what you have to say, not what you ought. Any truth is better than make-believe.

—Henry David Thoreau

Tell the truth. It seems so simple, and yet we continually have to be reminded. What are we trying to hide? Did Adam and Eve have to hide themselves from God after they committed the first sin by eating the apple?

My son, do not forget my law, but let your heart keep my commands; for length of days and long life and peace they will add to you. Let not mercy and truth forsake you; bind them around your neck, write them on the tablet of your heart, and so find favor and high esteem in the sight of God and man. Trust in the Lord with all your heart, and lean not on your own understanding; in all your ways

acknowledge Him, and He shall direct your paths.
(Proverbs 3:1–6)

Must one tie a string on one's finger to stay on the right path? Lies are one of the abominations of the Lord. "A proud look, a lying tongue, hands that shed innocent blood, a heart that devises wicked plans, feet that are swift in running to evil, a false witness who speaks lies, and one who sows discord among brethren" (Proverbs 6:17–19). Be honest, search for truth, and share with others. That sounds so simple, but it gets complicated so quickly. When I hold my tongue, am I being kind or cowardly? Is it wrong to tell a little white lie, especially if the truth hurts? Some people seem to get away with crude speech whereas others with good intentions are called out because the listener heard from a different lens than the speaker. According to Henry David Thoreau, perhaps we should say it anyway as long as it is the truth. I would amend it to say that we should speak the truth unless that truth does nothing but harm those who are listening. This is similar to a saying that my dad often repeated, "If you can't say something nice about someone, then say nothing at all." My dad was a very quiet man, so I listened carefully whenever he spoke. His words were full of wisdom. We should refrain from saying anything harmful and only use words that further God's kingdom. We should be instruments of truth and peace.

The truth can hurt, and it is not always apparent to the speaker. I tend to be a little too honest at times, at least according to my husband. I am afraid that my son inherited that trait from me. Perhaps that came from our German heritage. Germans tend to speak their minds without any sugar coating. Greg was honest from an early age. I remember one time when he was young. We were about to let him go out with friends when he reminded us that he was grounded. He remembered his punishment much better than me and was honest enough to remind me. I could always count on him to tell me the truth if asked the right questions. I remember another time when he had been involved in a fender bender during his senior year in high school. I asked him what he learned from the experience, hoping that he might say following too close or not paying attention to the road were good things to avoid. Instead, he commented on the Ford Geo and how badly it was damaged; he said he would never purchase a vehicle so poorly built. That was not what I wanted to hear, but my dear son was honest to a fault. Similarly, I used this trait that he inherited as my personal weakness during a job interview. I responded that my husband tells me that I can be too honest at times. He does often remind me of topics to stay away from when visiting certain people. He knows I sometimes blurt out the truth rather than considering the dynamics of the situation.

Jesus appears to be quite blunt with the truth in the gospels. He was not afraid to stir up controversy with the leaders of the church. His apostles were warned,

> Then Jesus said to them, "Take heed and beware of the leaven of the Pharisees and the Sadducees. … How is it you do not understand that I did not speak to you concerning bread? – but to beware of the leaven of the Pharisees and Sadducees." Then they understood that He did not tell them to beware of the leaven of bread, but of the doctrine of the Pharisees and Sadducees. (Matthew 16:6, 11–12)

Jesus was perhaps sugar coating at first, but His apostles often needed more blunt language. Further, Jesus was not afraid to speak the truth publicly as needed.

> Then Jesus spoke to the multitudes and to His disciples, saying: "The scribes and the Pharisees sit in Moses' seat. Therefore whatever they tell you to observe, that observe and do, but do not do according to their works; for they say, and do not

do. For they bind heavy burdens, hard to bear, and lay them on men's shoulders; but they themselves will not move them with one of their fingers." (Matthew 23:1–4)

I do not promote such open condemnation of sinful leaders without careful consideration of the consequences. Will any good come of it? If not, remain quiet. Perhaps our first action before such bold speech should be one of prayer, just as Jesus often did during His ministry to the crowds: "So He Himself often withdrew into the wilderness and prayed" (Luke 5:16).

The thing that amazed me most about Jesus' actions is that He always knew the needs of others. When friends went to great lengths to bring a sick man, He knew that the greater need was forgiveness of sins.

> When Jesus saw their faith, He said to the paralytic, "Son, your sins are forgiven you." And some of the scribes were sitting there and reasoning in their hearts, "Why does this Man speak blasphemies like this? Who can forgive sins but God alone?" But immediately, when Jesus perceived in His spirit that they reasoned thus within themselves, He said to them, "Why do you reason about these things in your hearts? Which is easier, to say to the paralytic, your sins are forgiven you, or to say, arise, take up your bed and walk? But that you may know that the Son of Man has power on earth to forgive sins," - He said to the paralytic, "I say to you, arise, take up your bed, and go to your house." Immediately he arose, took up the bed, and went out in the presence of them all, so that all were amazed and glorified God, saying, "We never saw anything like this!" (Mark 2:5–12)

He always knew what they needed to hear. Sometimes they needed nothing more than what they already had, "'Heal the sick, cleanse the lepers, raise the dead, cast out demons. Freely ye have received, freely give. Provide neither gold nor silver nor copper in your money belts, nor bag for your journey, nor two tunics, neither sandals, nor staffs; for a worker is worthy of his food'" (Matthew 10:8–10). Jesus knew that their needs would be provided. What will your response be when you hear God's small voice to go forth in ministry to the world? Will you be bold with the truth? Will you pray before you speak, making sure your words will be said in spirit and truth, with compassion for the needs of the hearer?

It crosses my mind at times, especially as I have read through the gospels, that there is a sermon in every verse of the Bible. It is a wealth of wisdom for us. There is also something in the Bible for our every need. I cannot think of one crisis in my life where the Bible did not have wisdom I needed to hear. My husband, David, has never shied away from sharing God's word with others. He is not a professional but has filled in for others when they had to be absent from the pulpit. One thing I have learned from leading Bible studies and preparing devotionals is that I often learn much more as the leader than I often get when participating in programs given by others. We often share in areas where we still need more perfection through God's grace in our lives.

> The Lord is my light and my salvation; whom shall I fear? The Lord is the strength of my life; of whom shall I be afraid? When the wicked came against me to eat up my flesh, my enemies and foes, they stumbled and fell. Though an army may encamp against me, my heart shall not fear; though war may rise against me, in this I will be confident. One thing I have desired of the Lord, that will I seek: that I may dwell in the house of the Lord all the days of my life, to behold the beauty of the

Lord, and to inquire in His temple. For in the time of trouble He shall hide me in His pavilion; in the secret place of His tabernacle He shall hide me; He shall set me high upon a rock. And now my head shall be lifted up above my enemies all around me; therefore I will offer sacrifices of joy in His tabernacle; I will sing, yes, I will sing praises to the Lord. Hear, O Lord, when I cry with my voice! Have mercy also upon me, and answer me. When You said, "Seek My face," my heart said to You, "Your face, Lord, I will seek." Do not hide Your face from me; do not turn your servant away in anger; You have been my help; do not leave me nor forsake me, O God of my salvation. When my father and my mother forsake me, then the Lord will take care of me. Teach me Your way, O Lord, and lead me in a smooth path, because of my enemies. Do not deliver me to the will of my adversaries; for false witnesses have risen against me, and such as breathe out violence. I would have lost heart, unless I had believed that I would see the goodness of the Lord in the land of the living. Wait on the Lord; be of good courage, and He shall strengthen your heart; wait, I say, on the Lord! (Psalm 27:1–14)

– ❧ –

Key Bible Verses: Exodus 4:10–12, Psalm 25:2–5, Luke 12:7–12, Hebrews 5:1–14, Titus 2:1–15

Keywords: Afraid, faith, light, preach, salt, teach(ing)

Song: "On Christ the Solid Rock" (We all need to stand on the solid and unchanging ground, which is the truth of our Lord and Master.)

Old Testament command: "You shall not bear false witness against your neighbor" (Exodus 20:16)

Questions:

1. What is one thing valued by the world but not the heavens?

2. What is one worldly joy that would be hard to give up?

3. What is one statement of truth that a friend of yours needs to hear? Or that you could post on social media?

Ponderable:

Honesty does not seem negotiable, but what if the truth hurts—really hurts? Why was Jesus reluctant to admit His position? Was He trying to save Himself? The crucifixion story is in all four gospels: Matthew 26–27, Mark 14–15, Luke 22–23, and John 18. He spoke with questions like, "Why do you ask Me?" (John 18:21) and "Are you speaking for yourself about this, or did others tell you this concerning Me?" (John 18:34).

CHAPTER 12

Reflect on Your Spiritual Life

So Jesus said to him, "Why do you call me good?
No one is good but One, that is, God."

—Luke 18:19

Whenever you find yourself on the side of the
majority, it is time to pause and reflect.

—Mark Twain

Search others for their virtues, thyself for thy vices.

—Ben Franklin

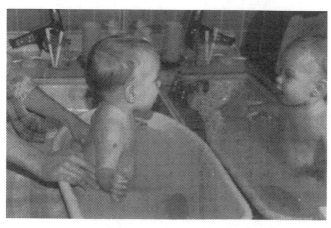

A reflection of my baby

Ponder; think about the life you lead. Reflect on your spirituality. Are there contradictions between your life and Christian teachings? Where are you in your life journey? When you consider your life, is it good enough? Can we ever be good enough to earn eternal life and happiness? When Jesus said that the gate to eternal life was narrow, does that mean only 25 percent or even fewer make it? The quote by Mark Twain suggests a number less than 50 percent. What is your score? Wouldn't it be nice if we had an app on our phone to give us our current score and whether that score was good enough for the final cut? We must reflect on our lives. Sometimes our reflections are clearer than others, similar to the reflection I was able to capture on the train as it went through a tunnel. In our earlier days, as with the picture of my firstborn, our reflections may be easier to look at. Of course, babies and puppies are always cuter in pictures than grownups. As we go through life, we should constantly consider where we are in our relationship with God.

As a teacher, I was expected to test my students. I was not perfect, but I always did my best to be fair. Ultimately, there was a cutoff score for each course that determined if one passed or failed. In public school, each course required a curriculum, instruction, and assessment. As a Christian in this world, I would argue that our curriculum is the Bible. It is our only written correspondence from our final assessor to determine our acceptability for eternal life. Our instruction can be done through reading, but correspondence and online courses are not as effective as face-to-face instruction, which for Christians means active participation in a church. On the other hand, you are on your own for your assessment unless you want to roll the dice and let the final exam become your only assessment. Frequent and honest self-assessments should be done on a regular schedule, hopefully more often than at New Year's, when resolutions are made. Even though you may not know the cutoff score, you can self-assess to determine areas where you could improve.

Self-assessment is not easy without guidelines, and the best-known guidelines for Christians are the Ten Commandments.

However, the rich young ruler was not "complete" with just obedience to the Jewish laws. Jesus is able to look inside our hearts. Where is your heart? Do you put God above the pleasures of the world? All of the time? How well do you practice submission and obedience to Jesus Christ? Jesus wants your mind, body, spirit, and strength. Mind: do you accept Jesus as your Lord and Savior? Body: are you obedient to God's commands? Spirit: are you aware of God's design for your life? Strength: do you put your time and energy into God's work or the earthly desires of the world? No one can ever measure up to the standards of the Master. We will never be complete and will always have room for improvement, but that does not give us an excuse for not trying.

We must choose to live in the spirit, not the flesh.

> For you, brethren, have been called to liberty; only do not use liberty as an opportunity for the flesh, but through love serve one another. For all the law is fulfilled in one word, even in this: "You shall love your neighbor as yourself." But if you bite and devour one another, beware lest you be consumed by one another! I say then: walk in the Spirit, and ye shall not fulfil the lust of the flesh. For the flesh lusts against the Spirit, and the Spirit against the flesh; and these are contrary to one another, so that you do not do the things that you wish. But if you are led by the Spirit, you are not under the law. Now the works of the flesh are evident, which are: adultery, fornication, uncleanness, lewdness, Idolatry, sorcery, hatred, contentions, jealousies, outbursts of wrath, selfish ambitions, dissensions, heresies, envy, murders, drunkenness, revelries, and the like; of which I tell you beforehand, just as I also told you in time past, that those who practice such things will not inherit the kingdom of God. But the

fruit of the Spirit is love, joy, peace, longsuffering, kindness, goodness, faithfulness, gentleness, self-control. Against such there is no law. And those who are Christ's have crucified the flesh with its passions and desires. If we live in the Spirit, let us also walk in the Spirit. Let us not become conceited, provoking one another, envying one another. (Galatians 5:13–26)

Thank goodness that God gives us according to His goodness and not according to what we deserve. We do not deserve anything. We cannot earn eternity. Eternal life is freely given by grace through faith. God's mercy hands eternal life to us with an open hand, but we must accept it and receive it every day.

– ⧼ –

Key Bible Verses: Jeremiah 31:37, Luke 6:27–38, Mark 7:36–37, Ephesians 4:4–7

Keyword: Measure

Song: "I Don't Deserve This"

This is an original by yours truly. As you can tell, I am not a professional songwriter. It could use a professional's touch.

Tests/Questioning in the Bible

> Now it came to pass after these things that God tested Abraham, and said to him, "Abraham!" And he said, "Here I am." Then He said, "Take now your son, your only son Isaac, whom you love, and go to the land of Moriah, and offer him there as a burnt

offering on one of the mountains of which I shall tell you." So Abraham rose early in the morning and saddled his donkey, and took two of his young men with him, and Isaac his son; and he split the wood for the burnt offering, and arose and went to the place of which God had told him. (Genesis 22:1–3)

Then one of them, a lawyer, asked Him a question, tempting Him, and saying, "Teacher, which is the great commandment in the law?" Jesus said to him, "You shall love the Lord your God with all your heart, with all your soul, and with all your mind. This is the first and great commandment. And the second is like it: You shall love your neighbor as yourself. On these two commandments hang all the Law and the Prophets." While the Pharisees were gathered together, Jesus asked them, saying, "What do you think about the Christ? Whose Son is He?" They said to Him, "The Son of David." He said to them, "How then does David in the Spirit call Him Lord, saying: The Lord said to my Lord, sit at My right hand, till I make Your enemies Your footstool? If David then call Him Lord, how is He his Son?" And no one was able to answer Him a word, nor from that day on did anyone dare question Him anymore. (Matthew 22:35–46)

I know your works, that you are neither cold nor hot. I could wish you were cold or hot. So then, because you are lukewarm, and neither cold nor hot, I will vomit you out of My mouth. Because you say, I am rich, have become wealthy, and have need of nothing—and do not know that you are wretched, miserable, poor, blind, and naked. (Revelation 3:15–17)

Questions:

1. The Bible is full of people who were able to do much more than humanly possible because God worked through them. Which Bible heroes do you relate to best?

2. What was their weakness? What is your weakness?

3. As you consider the commands of God and reflect on your own actions, what Bible verse is most helpful in motivating you to follow God's intentions for your life?

Ponderable:

Why is it so much easier to see the faults in others than in ourselves? That may be a major cause of the incivility in politics today. It is so hard to accept that good people disagree with our own beliefs.

And why do you look at the speck in your brother's eye, but do not consider the plank in your own eye? Or how can you say to your brother, "Let me remove the speck from your eye"; and look, a plank is in your own eye? Hypocrite! First remove the plank from your own eye, and then you will see clearly to remove the speck from your brother's eye. (Matthew 7:3–5)

CHAPTER 13

Live a Good Life

"Good Teacher, what good thing shall I do that I may obtain eternal life?" So He said to him, "Why do you call Me good? No one is good but One, that is God. But if you want to enter into life, keep the commandments." He said to Him, "Which ones?" Jesus said, "You shall not commit murder, you shall not commit adultery, you shall not steal, you shall not bear false witness, honor your father and your mother, and you shall love your neighbor as yourself." The young man said to Him, "All these things I have kept from my youth. What do I still lack?" Jesus said to him, "If you want to be perfect, go, sell what you have and give to the poor, and you will have treasure in heaven; and come, follow Me." But when the young man heard that saying, he went away sorrowful, for he had great possessions.
—Matthew 19:16–22 (Parallel passages in Mark 10:17–22 and Luke 18:18–23)

There is only One who is good. We can never be good enough to earn what God has in store for us in heaven. How then should we live? Sometimes I long for clear and plain directions from God as to what I should do. But we must be very careful about what we wish for, because I soon realize that I would be in big trouble, like the rich young man who went away grieved. If God gives us clear instructions, then we must obey or else face eternal anguish. We can never be good enough for the treasures in heaven, but by the grace of God, we can be forgiven if we only open the door and ask, then do our best to follow Jesus' example.

Historically, the commandments for living have been the Ten Commandments from the Old Testament. As I studied the gospels, I found that the Ten Commandments were amazingly consistent with Jesus' teachings. He did not come to abolish the old law but to fulfill it. As I analyzed the teachings of Jesus, I realized that the law and the prophets were a good starting point for living a good life. The Ten Commandments tell us what we should do. However, they are not enough to earn our treasure in heaven. Jesus fulfilled these commands by asking His disciples to take them to heart, to move from doing to caring. Chapters 2 through 11 all match one of the Ten Commandments, but with the additional compassion of our Lord and Savior, Jesus Christ. If we choose God as the master of our lives, then we must go beyond the *shall nots* of the old commandments and embrace the giving and healing heart as followers and disciples of Christ.

My journey in life does not end with retirement and the acquisition of a doctoral degree. It won't even be over at the end of my earthly life, for it is then that my next and more glorious life will begin. I still have a long way to go to complete my life so God will one day say, "Well done, good and faithful servant" (Matthew 25:23). At least I am hoping to hear those words from my Lord and Master. I really did not deserve anything that I have received in this life, and the next will be better than anything I could ever imagine. Thank God!

– ⊙ –

This is Jesus' special prayer for His followers to be One in spirit with one another as well as the Father, Son, and Holy Spirit:

> Jesus spoke these words, lifted up His eyes to heaven, and said: "Father, the hour has come. Glorify Your Son, that Your Son also may glorify You, as You have given Him authority over all flesh, that He should give eternal life to as many as You have given Him. And this is eternal life, that they may know You, the only true God, and Jesus Christ whom You have sent. I have glorified You on the earth. I have finished the work which You have given Me to do. And now, O Father, glorify Me together with Yourself, with the glory which I had with You before the world was.
>
> "I have manifested Your name to the men whom You have given Me out of the world. They were Yours, You gave them to Me, and they have kept Your word. Now they have known that all things which You have given Me are from You. For I have given to them the words which You have given Me; and they have received them, and have known surely that I came forth from You, and they have believed that You sent Me.
>
> "I pray for them. I do not pray for the world but for those whom You have given Me, for they are Yours. And all Mine are Yours, and Yours are Mine, and I am glorified in them. Now I am no longer in the world, but these are in the world, and I come to You. Holy Father, keep through Your name those whom You have given Me, that they may be one as We are. While I was with them in the world, I kept them in Your name. Those whom You gave Me I have kept; and none of them is lost except the son

of perdition, that the scripture might be fulfilled. But now I come to You, and these things I speak in the world, that they may have My joy fulfilled in themselves. I have given them Your word; and the world has hated them because they are not of the world, just as I am not of the world. I do not pray that You should take them out of the world, but that You should keep them from the evil one. They are not of the world, just as I am not of the world. Sanctify them by Your truth. Your word is truth. As You sent Me into the world, I also have sent them into the world. And for their sakes I sanctify Myself, that they also may be sanctified by the truth.

"I do not pray for these alone, but also for those who will believe in Me through their word; that they all may be one, as You, Father, are in Me, and I in You; that they also may be one in Us, that the world may believe that You sent Me. And the glory which You gave Me I have given them, that they may be one just as We are One: I in them, and You in me; that they may be made perfect in one, and that the world may know that You have sent Me, and have loved them as You have loved me.

"Father, I desire that they also whom You gave Me may be with Me where I am, that they may behold My glory which You have given Me; for You loved Me before the foundation of the world. O righteous Father! The world has not known You, but I have known You; and these have known that You sent Me. And I have declared to them Your name, and will declare it, that the love with which You loved Me may be in them, and I in them." (John 17:1–26)

– ❧ –

Key Bible Verses:

Jeremiah 17:5: "Thus says the Lord: cursed is the man who trusts in man and makes flesh his strength, whose heart departs from the Lord."

John 15:17: "These things I command you, that you love one another."

Revelation 22:14: "Blessed are those who do his commandments, that they may have the right to the tree of life, and may enter through the gates into the city."

Keywords: Command(ed/ment/ments)

Song: "I Can Only Imagine" (a favorite song of mine even before the movie)

Questions:

1. As noted above, many people share their wisdom. What is one of your most inspirational quotes for living a good life?

1. Who, historical or personal, inspires you to live well? What commands are evident in their life?

1. What one thing might Jesus ask you to do to be complete and have treasure in heaven?

Ponderable:

Many learned and well-respected people share their wisdom with the world. You have just read my wisdom, starting with choosing well. What words of wisdom would you share with the world?

Bibliography

Bronfenbrenner, Urie. *The Ecology of Human Development.* Cambridge, MA: Harvard University Press, 1979.

Charmaz, Kathy. *Constructing Grounded Theory.* Los Angeles, CA: Sage, 2014.

Cole, R. Alan. *Mark.* Downers Grove, IL: InterVarsity Press, 1989.

Dewey, John. *Democracy and Education.* Scottsdale, AZ: Simon & Brown, 2011.

Dweck, Carol S. *Mindset.* New York, NY: Ballantine Books, 2006.

Gideons International. *New Testament.* Nashville, TN: National Publishing Company, 1974.

Glaser, Barney G. & Strauss, Anselm L. *The Discovery of Grounded Theory: Strategies for Qualitative Research.* Hawthorne, NY: Aldine Publishing Company, 1967.

Krznaric, Roman. *How Should We Live?* Katonah, NY: BlueBridge, 2011.

LeVay, Simon. *Gay, Straight, and the Reason Why.* Oxford, NY: Oxford University Press, 2017.

Lewis, C. S. *Mere Christianity*. Westwood, NJ: Barbour and Company, 1952.

Morgan, Robert J. *Then Sings My Soul*. Nashville, TN: Thomas Nelson, 2003.

Robison, Betty. *Women at the Well: 32 Refreshing Devotions for a Thirsty Soul*. Fort Worth, TX: LIFE Outreach, 2003.

Sheldon, Charles M. *In His Steps*. Westwood, NJ: Barbour and Company, 1985.

Shore, John. *Unfair*. Columbia, SC: John Shore, 2013.

Strong, James, *The Exhaustive Concordance of the Bible*. Peabody, MA: Hendrickson, n.d.

Swain, Carol M. *Be the People*. Nashville, TN: Thomas Nelson, 2011.

Zondervan Corporation. *The Comparative Study Bible*. Grand Rapids, MI: Zondervan, 1984.

Acknowledgments

I must thank my Lord and Savior most of all for the blessings and opportunities I have received. I feel very blessed to live in a great country, in a good Christian family, with a good education, and with a super husband. I credit the PhD program in leadership studies at the University of Central Arkansas (UCA) with training in qualitative analysis. I was blessed to be surrounded by a great group of kind and caring university faculty at UCA.

The inspiration for this book actually came from a student of mine, Madison Breazeale. When she wrote her honors thesis at UCA, I could imagine it expanded into a book. In her paper, she shared how Jesus' teaching methods match many of the best practices for teachers today. Her idea of using the gospels as a primary source inspired me to use the gospels for my research question of how one should live a good life.

-My final thank you goes to my dear family, especially my husband. Without their love and support, I would not be me. Thank you, David, and my children, Greg, Tina, and April. I love you more than you will ever know.

My final inspiration came from my fourteen grandchildren. I must share one sweet comment for each one, starting with the youngest. I cannot wait to get to know Felix (Cookie). Sharron Ritarose (Jellybean) is a tiny girl with a big heart. Peter Stanley has stolen my heart because he reminds me of my dad. Elijah was born on All Saints Day; need I say more. George is my roomie; he helps me get things done. I love going places with Nicholas; he is such a good listener. Veronica Jane is a complex, beautiful, animal-loving child. Madeline is so insightful and caring. Faye is such a strong-willed girl who will only be limited by her own imaginations. Maramarie is a beautiful and smart dancer. Doc is a determined young man with a big heart. Mary Ella is a strong and kind young lady. Tyler is such a friendly young man; I love your hugs. Last, but not least, is my school and DAR buddy, Alana.

Appendix A: Occurrences of Key Words in the Gospels Using Strong's Exhaustive Concordance

Chapter	Keyword	Matthew (28)	Mark (16)	Luke (24)	John (21)	Sum
1	**Seek**					
1	Fulfil (led)	2 (16)	0 (4)	0 (8)	0 (11)	41
1	Ghost	7	6	12	5	30
1	Law	11	0	14	15	40
1	Prophet(s)	23 (17)	4 (4)	14 (18)	10 (4)	94
1	Scripture(s)	0 (4)	2 (2)	1 (3)	11 (1)	24
1	Spirit(s)	10 (3)	17 (4)	21 (6)	17 (0)	78
1	Tradition	3	5	0	0	8
1	Word(s)	19 (6)	13	20	22	74
1	Written	10	8	17	4	39
2	**Choose**					
2	Eternal	2	3	2	9	16
2	Follow(ed)	6 (20)	7 (13)	9 (11)	9 (5)	80
2	Hear	25	15	24	18	82
2	Kingdom	55	20	44	5	124
2	Master(s)	16 (2)	16 (0)	24 (1)	10 (0)	69
2	See	33	17	36	37	123

2	Serve	3	0	9	2	14
3	**Glorify**					
3	Good	39	12	29	10	90
3	Glorify(ed)	1 (2)	0 (1)	0 (6)	9 (12)	31
3	Glory	9	3	12	11	35
3	Worship(ed)(ing)	5 (8) (1)	1 (2) (0)	3 (1) (0)	9 (2) (0)	32
4	**Revere**					
4	Name	18	12	22	23	75
5	**Sabbath**					
5	Ask	12	7	13	17	49
5	Fast	7	6	4	0	17
5	Honor	4	3	1	10	18
5	Pray	12	8	14	5	39
5	Sabbath	10	11	18	11	50
5	Wait	0	1	2	0	3
5	Watch	10	8	4	0	22
6	**Virtue**					
6	Body	15	6	13	5	39
6	Bridegroom	6	3	2	3	14
6	Flesh	5	4	2	12	23
6	Holy	11	7	19	5	42
6	Temple	20	12	19	14	65
7	**Family**					
7	Chosen	3	1	2	5	11
7	Father	60	19	41	124	244
7	Mother	28	19	21	9	77
8	**Ordain**					
8	Authority	6	7	9	1	23
8	Baptize(ed)(ing)	2 (8) (1)	2 (8) (0)	2 (7) (0)	2 (5) (3)	40

8	Peace	6	8	19	5	38
8	Power	8	7	18	7	40
8	Repent	2	2	4	0	8
8	Reward	13	1	3	0	17
9	**Give**					
9	Bread	14	14	14	20	62
9	Fruit	15	8	13	10	46
9	Give	36	16	43	24	119
9	Heart	15	10	12	7	44
9	Water	7	4	7	24	42
10	**Heal**					
10	Forgive	8	6	7	0	21
10	Heal(ed)	5 (10)	2 (6)	8 (17)	2 (1)	51
10	Judge	4	0	8	11	23
10	Kill	9	5	6	9	29
11	**Truth**					
11	Afraid	7	7	5	4	23
11	Faith	12	5	12	0	29
11	Light	14	1	13	23	51
11	Preach	4	4	6	0	14
11	Salt	2	3	1	0	6
11	Teach(ing)	4 (6)	4 (3)	2 (5)	3 (0)	27
12	**Reflect**					
12	Measure	2	4	2	1	9
13	**Conclude**					
13	Command(ed)	3 (10)	1 (10)	3 (9)	2 (1)	39
13	Commandment(s)	5 (4)	5 (3)	2 (2)	7 (4)	32

Appendix B: Gospel References to the Old Testament

Genesis 2:24: "Therefore a man shall leave his father and mother and be joined to his wife, and they shall become one flesh." (Referenced in Matthew 19:5, Mark 10:7.)

Deuteronomy 6:5: "You shall love the Lord your God with all your heart, with all your soul, and with all your strength." (Referenced in Matthew 22:37–39, Mark 12:28–34, Leviticus 19:18.)

Deuteronomy 6:13: "You shall fear the Lord your God and serve Him, and shall take oaths in His name." (Referenced by Matthew 4:10, Luke 4:8.)

Deuteronomy 6:16: "You shall not tempt the Lord your God as you tempted Him in Massah." (Referenced by Matthew 4:7, Luke 4:12.)

Deuteronomy 8:3: "So He humbled you, allowed you to hunger, and fed you with manna which you did not know nor did your fathers know, that He might make you know that man shall not live by bread alone; but man lives by every word that proceeds from the mouth of the Lord." (Referenced by Matthew 4:4, Luke 4:4)

Psalm 8:2: "Out of the mouth of babes and nursing infants You have ordained strength, because of Your enemies, that You may silence the enemy and the avenger." (Referenced by Matthew 21:16)

Psalm 118:22–23: "The stone which the builders rejected has become the chief cornerstone. This was the Lord's doing; it is marvelous in our eyes." (Referenced by Matthew 21:42, Mark 12:10–11, Luke 20:17.)

Isaiah 6:9–10: "And He said, 'Go, and tell this people: keep on hearing, but do not understand; keep on seeing, but do not perceive. Make the heart of this people dull, and their ears heavy, and shut their eyes; lest they see with their eyes, and hear with their ears, and understand with their heart, and return and be healed.'" (Referenced by Matthew 13:14–15, Mark 4:12, Luke 8:10, John 12:40.)

Isaiah 29:13: "But the word of the Lord was to them, 'Precept upon precept, precept upon precept, line upon line, line upon line, here a little, there a little.' That they might go and fall backward, and be broken and snared and caught." (Referenced by Matthew 15:7–9, Mark 7:6–7.)

Isaiah 40:3–5: "The voice of one crying in the wilderness: 'Prepare the way of the Lord; make straight in the desert a highway for our God. Every valley shall be exalted and every mountain and hill brought low; the crooked places shall be made straight and the rough places smooth; the glory of the Lord shall be revealed, and all flesh shall see it together; for the mouth of the Lord has spoken.'" (Referenced by Luke 3:4–6, John 1:23.)

Isaiah 53:1: "Who has believed our report? And to whom has the arm of the Lord been revealed?" (Referenced by John 12:38.)

Isaiah 61:1–2: "The Spirit of the Lord God is upon Me, because the Lord has anointed Me to preach good tidings to the poor; He has sent Me to heal the brokenhearted, to proclaim liberty to the captives, and the opening of the prison to those who are bound; to proclaim the acceptable year of the Lord, and the day of vengeance of our God; to comfort all who mourn." (Referenced by Luke 4:17–19, 21.

Hosea 6:6: "For I desire mercy and not sacrifice, and the knowledge of God more than burnt offerings." (Referenced by Matthew 9:13, Matthew 12:7.)

Malachi 3:1: "Behold, I send My messenger, and he will prepare the way before Me. And the Lord, whom you seek, will suddenly come to His temple, even the Messenger of the covenant, in whom you delight. Behold, He is coming,' says the Lord of hosts." (Referenced by Matthew 11:10, Mark 1:2, Luke 7:27.)

Zechariah 13:7: "'Awake, O sword, against My Shepherd, against the Man who is My Companion,' says the Lord of hosts. 'Strike the Shepherd, and the sheep shall be scattered; then I will turn My hand against the little ones.'" (Referenced by Matthew 26:31, Mark 14:27.)

*A more expansive list can be found from Rich Robinson at https://jewsforjesus.org/answers/jesus-references-to-old-testament-scriptures/.

About the Author

Doctor Grammy (Dr. Mara Jane Cawein) is a retired educator, mother of 3, and grandmother of 14. She has a BS in Mathematics, MSE in Math Education, and PhD in Leadership Studies, all from the University of Central Arkansas. She was a computer software engineer, a high school mathematics teacher with national board certification, and a university instructor for educators and pre-service teachers. While on a college of education staff, she worked with pre-service teachers and national board candidates. She led state sites for non-traditional licensure and candidate support for teachers pursuing national board certification. She served on the board for Arkansas Teachers for National Board Certification (ATNBC). She has also assessed teacher candidate entries for the National Board for Professional Teacher Standards (NTBPS).

She is a member of Kappa Delta Pi (KDP), an international honor society in education. She served as counselor for the Pi Beta chapter, led sessions at multiple conferences, and volunteered to assist with scholarship selection. She was honored as a KDP Teacher of Honor. She also co-authored a chapter for a teacher leadership book published by KDP. She has served as a Sunday school teacher, youth director, attended numerous Bible study groups, and led many as well. Some of the topics of the special mission studies that she led include Native Americans, Haiti, and poverty.

As a member of the Daughters of the American Revolution (DAR), she has served as chapter treasurer, chapter regent, state historian, and state scholarship chair. DAR's motto is "God, home, and country". During her tenure as regent, her chapter's motto was "In God we trust."

Printed in the United States
By Bookmasters